# ODYSSEY OF
# COURAGE

Thank you for your
contribution to my life.

Affectionately

Halind Knoratiwala

*Praise for the book*

A fascinating account of the events and narratives that led to the making of Habil Khorakiwala—the person, and Wockhardt—the world-class institution that he built. An enjoyable retelling of how values were imbibed and shared, knowledge was acquired and imparted, mistakes were committed and resolved, and success was achieved and celebrated. It will inspire generations to come.

**Harsh Goenka**, Chairman, RPG Enterprises

This is the story of Wockhardt's evolution, under Habil Khorakiwala's leadership, from a family business to a research-led pharma company. This fascinating book captures personal, scientific and business development, chronicled against India's emergence as an economic powerhouse.

**David Livermore**, Professor of Medical Microbiology, University of East Anglia, UK

An inspiring saga of the rise of a research- and innovation-driven enterprise, with its roots firmly grounded in local soil, but with global footprints, and with many firsts to its credit. It vividly brings out what a visionary leader with 'yes we can' spirit can achieve with grit and determination.

**R.A. Mashelkar**, FRS; former Director General, CSIR; President, Indian National Science Academy

An astonishingly young Habil Khorakiwala intuited the need to build an Indian pharmaceutical company and take it to an international level...to establish a world-class Indian antibiotic research and development centre, at a time when no such institution existed in the country...at a time when big pharma had almost completely withdrawn from the field.

**Peter Appelbaum**, former Professor of Pathology, Hershey Medical School, Penn State University, USA

Habil took the company to great heights, in particular, to the regulated markets of Europe, the UK and the US. His achievements in the Indian pharmaceutical industry over the years have been outstanding. He has a deep sense of friendship, warmth and humour.

**Yusuf Hamied**, Chairman, Cipla

Habil Khorakiwala's journey of grit and gumption is the quintessential story of Indian pharma. A risk-taker at heart—the little boy who watched wide-eyed a frog getting dissected, and flaunted his Lambretta scooter in college—Habil took his company from Worli to the world, from formulations to drug discovery, hospitals and stem cells.

**Shekhar Gupta**, well-known Indian journalist

I learnt a lot from Habil during his tenure as the president of Federation of Indian Chambers of Commerce and Industry (FICCI) during the year 2006–07. We travelled together, across the world, for global conferences, business meetings, think-tank roundtables, scholarly seminars and engaging with the prime ministers and presidents of nations. I noticed that Habil had a special knack for garnering fresh ideas and new perspectives, with the motivation to convert some of these ideas into reality in the world of commerce and industry... He not only builds institutions and creates value, but also knows when to unlock the value and move on to a new challenge.

**Amit Mitra**, Finance Minister, West Bengal

Habil is a man of tremendous vision with a deep love for his family and passion for meeting the healthcare needs of his fellow countrymen and beyond.

**Craig K. Svensson**, Dean, College of Pharmacy, Purdue University, USA

# ODYSSEY OF
# COURAGE

The Story of an Indian Multinational

## HABIL KHORAKIWALA

MAVEN
RUPA

Published in Maven by
Rupa Publications India Pvt. Ltd 2017
7/16, Ansari Road, Daryaganj
New Delhi 110002

*Sales centres:*
Allahabad Bengaluru Chennai
Hyderabad Jaipur Kathmandu
Kolkata Mumbai

ISBN: 978-81-291-4895-7

First impression 2017

10 9 8 7 6 5 4 3 2 1

Printed and bound in India by Replika Press Pvt. Ltd.

*To Nafisa, with love;*
*to our children—Huzaifa, Murtaza and Zahabiya—with hope...*

# Contents

# Foreword

I love reading autobiographies. The writer can be a celebrity, a condemned politician, a business executive, a poet, a writer, a scientist, or even an ordinary citizen. I love getting a glimpse into the person's perspective on life, and their interpretation of events, persons, institutions, society and culture. I enjoy seeing the transformation in people and their environment, their passage from childhood to youth, their dealing with everyday life, and their reflections on life in hindsight. In many cases, it takes me to a world I might not have seen.

All autobiographies, no matter how they are written or structured, always give one an opportunity to see the passage of time, and see an entire universe encapsulated in one single person's life. It is a thrilling experience for any reader. I thank Habil Khorakiwala for allowing us this guided tour of history through his life.

How did I meet Khorakiwala? One of the rewards of my work has been the opportunity to discover and meet extremely successful people who also think about humanity, and Khorakiwala is one such committed individual. When I meet such people they always express their desire to do more. They take time to share their social concerns and commitments. Everyone has their own way of addressing their social concerns. I try to share with people the way I have tackled issues that move me. That chance meeting with Khorakiwala led to a lifelong connection between us.

In this book, Khorakiwala has given us a glimpse into the social history of Indian business and of the rise of technology- and science-based industry in India. This is also a historical documentation of society and economy as it evolved around him. He gives a stimulating account of how Wockhardt, a knowledge-based business, not only took root in a country far removed from such experiences, but also became a global player. Wockhardt's rise from its modest beginnings in the suburbs of Bombay (now Mumbai) to becoming a giant Indian multinational, with manufacturing and research centres in the United States and Europe and other parts of the world, is a thrilling story. A must-read for any entrepreneur, particularly in countries where almost all the ingredients for creating a global enterprise are missing.

Khorakiwala talks about his family and the support he received in the journey that started with one factory in a backward district of Maharashtra. He highlights his lifelong belief that not knowing cannot be grounds for not doing. He illustrates how he followed the path of learning instead of hiding behind the wall of dependency. Khorakiwala is a product of colonial economy education. But his story is about how he broke through the line, and defied the prevailing 'wisdom'.

In doing so, Khorakiwala became one of the pioneers of a new Indian pharmaceutical industry, which moved from being a local player to becoming a global leader. It changed lives and people—transformed scientists into believing in their capability to define the future of healthcare; transformed investors to think 'big' in terms of investing in science and technology enterprises; transformed policymakers to reorient the entire thinking behind those policies.

Khorakiwala's book coincides with Wockhardt turning fifty. I congratulate him for his contributions. And remind him that having achieved all that he narrates in the book, there is so much more to contribute. Keep marching the social march.

Professor Muhammad Yunus
Dhaka, Bangladesh
July 2017

## Chapter 1

# High Five

*Twenty years from now, you will be more disappointed by the things that you didn't do than by the ones you did do. So throw off the bowlines. Sail away from the safe harbour. Catch the trade winds in your sails. Explore. Dream. Discover.*

—Mark Twain

There is something about living by the sea. It injects a spirit of adventure. I grew up in Mumbai watching the sea and the sunsets. World over, coastal cities have harboured explorers, adventurers, merchants and mendicants. Seekers all. Those of us who live or work close to the sea cannot but look at it and think of the world beyond. That is what I was doing that Saturday afternoon in September of 1997, waiting for my visitor.

I was at my desk in my semicircular office overlooking the Arabian Sea on the fifth floor of Poonam Chambers in Worli. My visitor would be a gentleman known to me at the time only by his name and his impressive biodata. Mahesh Patel, or Mahesh as I call him now, had an impressive track record. He had by then worked for twenty-one long years at Hoechst, a German company that I held in high regard. He later joined Ranbaxy, an Indian pharmaceutical firm led then by its inspiring leader Parvinder Singh. Parvinder was a doyen of the Indian pharma industry. The elder son of Bhai Mohan Singh, a nationalist, a pioneer, a spirited business leader, Parvinder led Ranbaxy to great heights. Mahesh was, quite understandably, enthused enough by Parvinder's leadership and enterprise to join his quest for new drug discovery. Mahesh had specialized in the field of antibiotics.

I was convinced by then that antibiotics was where the future lay. However, it was not an easy decision to take whether I should be investing time and money in this direction. I had to do my bit of research about the business and the science of antibiotics before arriving at an informed decision. I found that antibiotics research was slowly turning into a quiet space with few serious players. This was after a heady growth phase that had lasted over four decades.

The journey to fight infections caused by bacteria, or microscopic living organisms, started a little over a decade after Alexander Fleming discovered, quite by accident, penicillin in his laboratory in London in 1928. The story goes that in an effort to understand the bacteria, he needed to culture or grow them. One day, before leaving for a vacation, he left these in his laboratory. When he returned he found that a fungus had grown in the bacterial plate and saw a clear margin around the fungus. The bacteria was not growing around the margin. On examination, he found that this was because the fungus was producing penicillin and it was doing so to protect itself against the bacteria. That led to the discovery of penicillin.

The majority of antibiotics have a natural origin. Some, like quinolones and sulpha drugs, are man-made. Bacteria have been around for millions of years and have self-protection mechanisms, which protect them from getting killed by other bacteria or fungus. This mechanism is what we call antibiosis. So, how does the antibiotic act? Every antibiotic kills bacteria in different ways, each has a different target or a site in the molecular structure of the bacteria that it attacks. Quinolones, for instance, act on the DNA replication machinery essential for the bacteria to grow and divide. Penicillin and cephalosporins act on the bacteria's cell wall, which is a rigid layer that protects the bacteria from the external environment. Typically, an antibiotic is said to be acting on a bacteria when it inhibits the functioning of the target it is meant to attack, making it difficult for the bacteria to live.

When a bacteria develops resistance, it either modifies the target structure or produces enzymes that make the drug ineffective. The antibiotic therefore is not able to do anything to the changed structure of its target. This is why when a drug that could cure a cough or cold is no longer able to offer relief, one must move to a higher level of antibiotic.

Matters get complicated when certain types of bacteria also have the ability to transfer the resistance genes to other bacteria. It is therefore important that patients are advised to avoid overuse and misuse of antibiotics. One must use the drug only when needed, in the correct dosage. Discontinuing administration of an antibiotic without completing the full course runs the risk of inducing drug resistance, with some bacteria still left to survive within the body.

The wide availability of penicillin during World War II, a few years after its discovery, helped save soldiers' lives. From then on to the 1980s a series of new antibiotics were discovered. About twenty-five different antibiotics belonging to five or six different classes were introduced in clinical use. Global multinational companies, including Pfizer, Glaxo, Merck, Eli Lilly, Smith, Kline & French (before the merger of SmithKline with Glaxo Wellcome) and Roche Hoechst & Abbott, helped expand the market year after year, introducing new drugs. These were all Western companies. Apart from the US, Germany, Switzerland, the UK and France, Japan was the other pioneer in pharma research. Indeed, it is often not recognized that Japan, which has a strong research-based pharma sector, has been an equally dynamic developer of new antibiotics. According to one estimate, the US, the EU and Japan together account for more than 90 per cent of global research and development (R&D) expenditure on drug discovery. Japan has had a strong commitment to research, and has developed as many as 282 new drugs since the turn of the century. Yet, only forty-four of them, barely 16 per cent, have been approved and marketed in Western Europe and US markets.

The risk aversion of Japanese pharma companies contrasts with their electronics and automobile companies, which have been so aggressive globally. I believe, Japan has lost a golden opportunity to dominate the global pharmaceutical landscape. Many of the blockbuster drugs introduced into global markets in the 1960s were originally Japanese innovations like levofloxacin (from Daiichi and administered in cases of urinary tract infections and pneumonia), tazobactam (from Taisho Pharmaceutical, this drug is always administered along with piperacillin in cases of serious bloodstream and urinary tract infections), clarithromycin (also from Taisho) and cefepime (from Meiji Seika). More recent examples include ceftaroline (Takeda) and ceftolozane (Fujisawa). Levofloxacin alone has been more than a billion-dollar product. Companies associated with these drugs today are Johnson & Johnson (for levofloxacin), Wyeth (now part of Pfizer, for tazobactam), Abbott (forclarithromycin) and Bristol-Myers Squibb (for cefepime).

As I write, I am aware that the Swiss multinational Roche is developing nacubactam, a product bought from the Japanese company Meiji Seika. Japanese pharma companies have developed many other drugs as well. However, they have remained content out-licensing the drugs they developed to Western companies. It is only recently that they have emerged as a force to reckon with globally, but they missed the great strategic opportunity to gain an early lead and global recognition during the post-war years.

It must be said to the credit of Indian entrepreneurship that even as many of our pharma companies operated mainly within the generics space, they made bold efforts to venture out and create a global business. The overseas market now accounts for 50 to 60 per cent of the turnover of most major Indian pharma companies. For Wockhardt, the world market has consistently had a share of over 50 per cent. Today Indian-made generics comprise 40 per cent of all US generic sales. The US is still the largest market in the world for pharma, including generics.

The world of drug discovery is a fascinating one and so has been its history and evolution. While at one end there are innovative drugs coming out of laboratories in Japan, at the other there are drugs discarded by multinational corporations (MNCs) that have found a niche market. For example, the Eli Lilly-discovered drug daptomycin, used for the so-called superbug Methicillin-Resistant Staphylococcus Aureus infection. The drug was initially sidelined and eventually almost discarded. It was sold to Cubist Pharmaceuticals, then a small US-based biopharmaceutical company. Cubist developed the drug, making it into a billion-dollar product, and the company eventually became such a powerhouse that when Merck bought it in 2014, it had to cough up close to $9 billion because of this product.

To me, the Cubist story illustrates that it is not just big scale and size but well-coordinated product development capabilities that make all the difference. The company not only developed the drug but also undertook its market development and transformed it into a billion-dollar product.

♋

In 1995, in order to get a first-hand feel of the MNC discovery research infrastructure and to discuss with their senior scientists I decided to visit the Sandoz facility in New Jersey, US, to meet up with Faizulla Kathawala, a Mumbaikar who had by then earned a global reputation for his invention of Lescol (fluvastatin sodium), a synthetic statin that was as effective as a natural statin. Statins are medicines that help lower the cholesterol level in blood. After completing his MS at the University of Bombay, Kathawala secured a PhD from a prestigious institution in Germany and by the time I was visiting him he was already one of the stars at Sandoz in the US.

He took me around the Sandoz facility and gave me a scientist's perspective on drug discovery. Many scientists spend a lifetime within the confines of acrid-smelling laboratories repeatedly iterating experiments and testing results with every change in the atomic structure. For years they may see no light at the end of the tunnel. Therefore, to keep themselves professionally relevant and abreast of the latest developments in their fields, they publish, attend conferences and keep the hope of discovery alive.

My visit to Sandoz gave me a good understanding of how to deal with scientists and researchers in a business enterprise. A modern business seeks results every year, indeed, every quarter and every month. It evaluates investment, expenditure, performance and almost every other business parameter on the basis of annual and quarterly results. Research cannot be conducted in such a straitjacketed manner. It is only after years of persistent work that, if one is lucky, a significant result would be forthcoming.

I believe that parameters like Key Performance and Result Areas (KPAs and KRAs) would have to be very differently specified for R&D in drug discovery as compared to our normal pharmaceutical manufacturing business.

My understanding of the discovery of novel drugs was further enhanced by my visit to Pfizer's research hub at Groton, Connecticut, in the US. Accompanying me on the trip to Groton were emerging leaders of Indian pharma, like Dilip Shanghvi, founder of Sun Pharma, and Prashant Tewari of US Vitamins (USV). At Groton, among other things, Pfizer was engaged in the discovery of new antibiotics. That visit provided me in-depth knowledge of the complexity of and the resources required for drug discovery.

Any drug discovery needs an extremely high level of commitment, which can come only from a deep understanding of that field. It also requires tonnes of patience and self-belief. Fortunately, I made the decision that Wockhardt needed to take that long and arduous path.

Coming to terms with multinationals' financial ability to invest in discovery research, given their deep pockets, made me uncomfortable. I was hoping at the time that Wockhardt would be able to invest in discovery research. How would we be able to compete with them on the same turf? Would we have the financial staying power? The changing priorities of MNCs with several of them vacating the antibiotics space, gave me some confidence.

I found part of the answer in an argument constantly put forth by my good friend, the late Kallam Anji Reddy, who was among the early birds in the antibiotics game in India, along with Parvinder Singh of Ranbaxy Laboratories. Both were highly committed and energetic entrepreneurs with a research orientation. They understood the science and the business of drug discovery.

By 1997, both had demonstrated the fact that the future of Indian pharma lay in product innovation based on original research. Anji Reddy would often tell me of the India advantage that we in pharma could bring in by focusing on the innovation-end of drug discovery, an area where our strengths lay. His view was that we had the talent, and innovation did not cost a fortune, in contrast to the drug development process. In addition to being hugely expensive, development, the other component of drug discovery, was fraught with stringent regulatory demands and high uncertainties. To overcome these challenges, he had devised the model of licensing out his drug candidates to global players with deep pockets.

⁓

Medicines, as the doctor will tell you, fall into two broad categories.

There are medicines that deal with acute ailments, like cancer, pain and infections, and there are those that deal with chronic ailments like diabetes and cardiovascular or heart-related problems. In the difference between these two kinds of medicines lie the business sense and an answer to why pharmaceutical companies are more drawn to chronic ailments. After all, for diabetes and heart problems, you need medicines for life. Since the demand for medicines for such ailments is long-term, by their very nature, these medicines tend to be more remunerative.

Within acute care, there are three areas where there is need for new medicines. One is pain, the other is cancer care and the third is anti-infectives or antibiotics. The problem with pain management is that the medication involves the use of controlled substances or psychotropic substances. We feel pain because wherever there is hurt, the nerve cells in the body pick up the signal and transmit it to the spinal cord and from there to the brain, which translates the message and conveys the feeling of pain. How do the nerve cells pick up the signals? Very simply, there are receptors called TrpV1 connected to nerve cells whose main job is to pick up the signals on what is happening elsewhere in the body. Pain-relieving medicines act on the receptors and affect the process of transmitting the message of pain to the brain and in the process, since they have an influence on mood and consciousness, they tend to be habit-forming. Therefore, this is an area that is fraught with regulatory challenges.

Cancer care is a rapidly growing segment of acute care. Several pharma companies, especially leading global companies, have been investing heavily in it. The US Food and Drug Administration (USFDA) data shows that there has been a gradual increase in the number of drugs being approved. Many companies have come to realize that they can get away with pricing cancer drugs high. While the stringency on drug toxicity is high for cancer drugs, it is surprising that the yardsticks to judge the side effects of antibiotics are even higher than for cancer drugs. I wonder if it has to do with the race to produce a wonder drug for cancer.

What I find interesting is that most MNCs have invested in the lucrative business of cancer care drugs, while vacating the antibiotics space. There has been a sharp decline in antibiotics drug discovery since the 1990s. Even Daiichi Sankyo recently announced its plan to shut down the antibiotics research work that was being done out of its Gurgaon (now Gurugram) unit in India. This is a sad end to what my friend Parvinder Singh started. He was so passionately committed to new drug discovery. Daiichi Sankyo had initially held on to this division even after their deal to give up their stake in Ranbaxy to Sun Pharma.

Part of this scale-down in antibiotics research is reflected in the gradual decline in the number of new drugs being approved by the USFDA in this space (Chart 1). For me, all of this meant not only that a new business opportunity had opened up for us, given our interest in new drug discovery, but also that this was happening in a market with declining competition. It was a bonus for me personally that this new business opportunity also offered us the chance to make use of our research, and allowed us to introduce new drugs into the market at a time when drug resistance was building up quite sharply.

I should hasten to add that all MNCs have not been oblivious of this opportunity. Roche, for example, has decided to return to antibiotics and they have restarted their efforts in this space. But in this kind of a research-based area, one cannot switch on and off when one likes. A programme once shut down takes a long time to effectively restart. Research is a pursuit in which one must remain committed over the long haul. So, despite their size and record, Roche will not have too many advantages in this field. I am confident that we can give them a run for their money.

Pharma research is, as I have said before, not merely expensive but it is also long drawn and needs an interdisciplinary approach. Research teams have to work together for long periods of time in a cooperative manner for them to find results. Building that team spirit itself takes a long time. Then, various disciplines have to work together and talk to each other and listen to each other. It is not just the data that has to do the talking. One must know how to synthesize and interpret the nuances of the findings in each discipline—microbiology and pharmacokinetics, the branch of pharmacology that is concerned with the movement of medicine within the body.

**Chart 1: Declining Antibacterial Approvals**

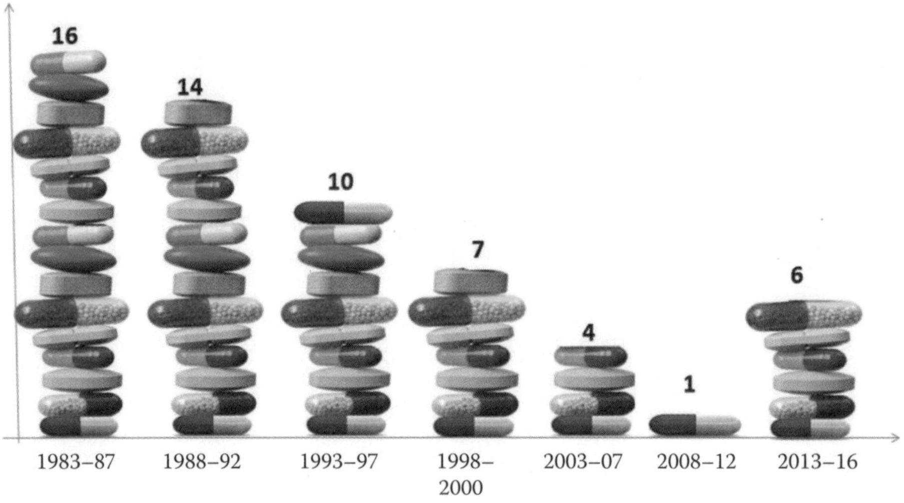

*NOTE: Majority of the new antibiotics introduced in the market since 2000 have targeted gram positive bacteria and, therefore, sufficient number of antibiotics for gram negative bacteria—which are more difficult to treat and cause higher number of infections— have not hit the market. Hence, two of Wockhardt's gram negative antibiotics—WCK 5222 and WCK 4282—are not just timely but will also address an important unmet medical need.*

Research possibilities in oncology also caught my attention because cancer care was becoming a huge unmet need. But then, I found every big pharma globally had a programme in cancer. They were also armed with the resources, deep domain knowledge in some cases and access to talent in this space abroad. So, within acute ailments, we were left with only antiinfective and a final question: should our research focus be on antibacterial medicines or on vaccines? This was easy to sort out. Taking the vaccines route meant going for a biological approach, which is a relatively less understood science than the chemistry approach we were good at. Also, at some stage, vaccines need to be mass-produced, which would again bring us into direct competition with big pharma.

Part of the reason for major MNCs vacating antibiotics was the emerging opportunity in chronic ailments, where newer drugs were being launched. Novo Nordisk, a leader in the fight against diabetes, was out with its first human insulin in 1982, a space that even we got into later, around 2003. But what went largely unsaid about antiinfectives or antibiotics was the inability of big pharma to develop novel approaches to deal with difficult-to-treat bacterial infections. This was despite more and more bacteria starting to evade the currently available antibiotics. But I am glad we still chose antibiotics. In many ways, we feel vindicated because the tide started turning from 2014. Some of these very companies were making a comeback into antibiotics. The most recent case being in August 2016, when Pfizer bought into the antibiotic business of AstraZeneca Plc.

❦

I believed our destiny was to find novel ways to kill bacteria. When I shared my thinking on this with Mahesh that Saturday afternoon in September, he broke into Gujarati and asked if I was willing to be a risk-taker and a long-distance runner. What was my philosophy on return on investment?

Investing in research in antibiotics in the hope of reaping commercial dividends required staying power and a willingness to concede defeat if one's labour bore no fruit. Investing in this space, Mahesh warned me, could well be like walking into a bottomless pit. Instead, parking funds in bank deposits was not a bad idea. In those days, banks offered a good 12 to 14 per cent rate of interest. As against this, antibiotics research meant no returns would be assured for a long time to come.

Hearing Mahesh, I could not help but laugh.

'You have a good sense of business', I told my scientist interlocutor. He was a fellow Gujarati after all. Business is in our genes, whatever our profession. 'Do not worry, I have done my homework. I am serious about this investment and I am willing to wait for the returns.'

Mahesh was not satisfied with that reply. 'How many people in your organization would the research team be reporting to?' he asked. Would he have to justify his research plans and spending to all manner of managers at various levels of the organization?

My reply was instant. 'Only me,' I assured him.

As I look back on that conversation two decades later, I am happy I said what I did. I am relieved that I had the staying power and faith in myself and my people. And to top it all, I am delighted I was able to hire the right people. Almost a year before Mahesh joined us in 1998, Noel J. D'Souza, a medicinal chemist, led the work in antibiotics. He continued to lead till he retired in 2003. Before D'Souza joined us, he had been deputy director of the Hoechst research centre and my guess is that he would have gone on to head it, had not Hoechst then followed the practice of always having a German lead. When D'Souza joined us, he had left Hoechst and was with Sun Pharma. We have come a long way since then and led by Mahesh, we today have a team of a hundred people in pre-clinical antibiotics research out of our facility in Aurangabad and close to thirty other people divided between India and the US involved in clinical research and handling regulatory matters. It gives me great satisfaction that none of them has chosen to leave us. Many of them began as young researchers. Continuity of personnel over a long period of time is a necessary requirement for research in pharma. We have been fortunate to have people like Mahesh and his multidisciplinary team for our drug discovery research.

That is the kind of investment in human capital and human relationships that a pharma company has to ensure to produce results. In fact, a year before he approached the age of retirement, Mahesh alerted me to the need to find a successor. I requested him to stay on; Mahesh continues to lead a very competent, creative and loyal R&D team.

I now know, with hindsight, that I invested well.

∽

I was committed to making Wockhardt a serious player in the field of antibiotics R&D and to this end, one of the most exciting and encouraging aspects was the profile of our drug candidates We could see the promise of novel approaches to the difficult-to-treat bacterial infections that were evading even some of the big global pharma companies Wockhardt's drug candidate 'zidebactam' is a first new class of gram negative antibiotic (medical jargon for bacteria whose outer membranes make them better equipped to evade the impact of the drugs) in 35 years. It is a new class of antibiotics known as 'betalactam enhancers'. That is, they not only help overcome the resistance to antibiotics but also synergistically boost the activity of antibiotics. To understand the significance of zidebactam, it may help to look at the trouble-causing infection landscape. Some of the organisms that need to be urgently dealt with include Acinetobacter (they cause hospital-acquired pneumonia and bloodstream infections) and Pseudomonas aeruginosa, which results in infections caused by burn injuries. Then, there are E.coli Klebsiella and Enterobacter, which all typically lead to urinary tract infections, intra-abdominal infections and hospital-acquired pneumonia. In fact, when E.coli, Klebsiella and Enterobacter become resistant to carbapenems, a class of drugs that is used as the last resort in serious infections, then these are called Carbapenem-Resistant Enterobacteriaceae (CRE). Zidebactam overcomes the multidrug-resistance mechanisms in gram negative superbugs, including the most dreaded mechanism called New Delhi Metallo β-lactamase (NDM), which renders the last line of antibiotics (carbapenems) ineffective.

Personally, it has been a fascinating journey for me. Understanding the nuances of drug discovery is critical here. While I cannot direct my team from a science perspective, I can certainly try and understand what is being done and get the feedback from external experts, which is what I have been doing for the last seven-odd years. I attended our first Key Opinion Leaders (KOL) meeting in Chicago in March 2012. KOL meetings are an important aspect of pharma research. Getting constant feedback from experts in the field is an essential part of the R&D process. The KOL meeting was attended by a range of renowned experts like Michael Jacobs of Case Western Research University, an authority on clinical microbiology; George Eliopoulous from the Harvard Medical School, an infectious disease specialist; and Karen Bush, a professor at Indiana University, Bloomington, who was formerly with Johnson & Johnson Pharmaceutical R&D. Karen is an expert in the mechanism of action of β-lactam and β-lactamase inhibitors. Then, there was Axel Dalhoff, who was formerly with Bayer and is a renowned microbiologist, and Robert A. Bonomo, who was the chief of medical service at the Louis Stokes Cleveland Department of Veterans Affairs Medical Center.

I sat back and observed. I was sceptical of getting a favourable opinion from the KOL on our programme because there was some initial hesitation on the part of some KOL members in accepting what we were saying. But, by the third and final day, the reservation had been converted into appreciation for the kind work we were doing. There was also appreciation for my personal involvement in the research programme. After that, I have not missed a single KOL meeting. These meetings have served to raise my confidence in my own team. Subsequently, in October 2015, I set up a Drug Discovery Governing Council that I chair to closely and regularly monitor the discovery programme and support the clinical development that follows. At the Governing Council meetings, I look at the target market for the drugs discovered by our team. This is important so we can decide which clinical studies to undertake and create a suitable product profile for the drug.

One of my major concerns has been about making drugs more accessible and affordable for the largest number of people in the developed and emerging markets. One way of making drugs accessible is to reduce the cost of manufacturing. But government support can also help. After all, lower healthcare costs can only reduce the pressure on the government's budget that higher incidence of ill-health causes. There are a few things that the government can easily do to help. First, it could tighten the diagnostic procedures in hospitals so that the drug is given only where it is required. Second, it could encourage bulk procurement of medicines to reduce overall cost. Finally, I am sure the industry would be happy to supply lower-cost drugs through public hospitals if the services offered by these hospitals are better targeted to the poor.

If we can develop a drug for the emerging markets, then we can also market it to the rest of the world. The need for antibiotics is high in emerging markets and consequently the market is huge, with three out of every four drugs sold in emerging markets, including India and China. Two of our five new drugs are specifically targeted at this patient audience. For example, we have Levonadifloxacin (WCK 771), an intravenous (IV) drug, and Alalevonadifloxacin, which is the oral version of the drug. Both these belong to the class of quinolones but with a difference. They are the first anti-MRSA products from the quinolones class of antibiotics. The MRSA is the world's first superbug.

15

Phase II studies are over in India and Phase III has begun in 2017. With Levonadifloxacin and Alalevonadifloxacin targeted at MRSA that causes infections like pneumonia and bloodstream infections in different parts of the body; there will now be both an oral and IV therapy route, which is not possible with the currently available drugs.

Another one of our drug candidates is nafithromycin, which belongs to the ketolides class of drugs. The hope it provides is in combating the multidrug-resistant (MDR) streptococcus pneumoniae, which causes pneumonia and a range of upper respiratory infections such as pharyngitis, middle ear infection, bronchitis and sinusitis. These can be deadly in terms of impact.

For example, in a single year, pneumococcal infections result in 1.6 million deaths worldwide, and more than 5 million people are hospitalized due to pneumococcal infections. In the US alone, pneumococci cause 1.2 million cases of infections. These MDR pathogens have been known to cause infections that may have in turn contributed to as many as 23,000 deaths in the US and 30,000 in Europe every year, and many more in developing countries, where the incidence of infectious diseases is much higher.

Nafithromycin is designed to stay longer in the lungs, and provide a shorter, more convenient once-a-day oral therapy, requiring just five days of treatment. Owing to its dual target in bacteria, it is highly effective against MDR pneumococci, against which common drugs like azithromycin, clarithromycin, erythromycin, tetracycline, penicillin, cephalosporin and sulphamethoxazole-trimethoprim are ineffective, particularly in children and elderly patients. When launched, nafithromycin will be a superior substitute to the current gold standard drug azithromycin.

Nafithromycin, or WCK 4873 as it is referred to internally, has commenced Phase II in the US and Europe for the treatment of community-acquired pneumonia. Phase I, which is performed on healthy volunteers, has been completed in the US. In Phase II, a drug is tried on patients. There are clearly two major spin-offs from this for Wockhardt. First, it has seen competition reduced with almost no other Indian company involved in this field of drugs. Even though at a global level there are some MNCs like Roche and Novartis making a re-entry into this space, the talent world has changed. With a thirty-year vacuum in discovery research in antibiotics, the skill sets have died down. The second spin-off is that Wockhardt nurtured skills and built its team. That is not all. More and more bright minds with international exposure are joining us.

David Friedland, for instance, who heads our clinical research in the US, joined us because we had a drug candidate like zidebactam. Then, in 2016, we had Jane Ambler join us, also in the US. She was last working with Merck, earlier with AstraZeneca and with Cubist and has experience in clinical microbiology. Our drug discovery programme has both breadth and depth. Few companies have really achieved these attributes through established in-house drug discovery programmes. In a recent analysis of our programme, McKinsey estimated a peak business potential of $2 billion.

৵

Given the work that we had been doing, it was with some degree of interest that I followed the decision of British Prime Minister David Cameron to constitute a commission, in July 2014, to review the problem of antimicrobial resistance. Done in collaboration with the Wellcome Trust, the review was chaired by Jim O'Neill, formerly chairman of Goldman Sachs. A professional economist, who also had a tenure in the British government, Jim O'Neill, or Lord O'Neill of Gatley, presented a paper, in May 2015, that examined the case for the development of new antibiotic drugs.

The O'Neill report emphasized the importance of ensuring the commercial viability of R&D in antibiotics. It recognized the need to attract bright minds to this field of research. The report endorsed the view of the World Health Organization that even though antibiotic resistance is the greatest challenge in infectious diseases, threatening rich and poor countries alike, '[...] so far it has not had nearly sufficient attention in terms of medical research.' It took the view that as a global public health threat, antibiotic resistance should arguably receive the same kind of public focus that HIV/AIDS had received in the 1990s or cancer research receives today—although it may not need the same level of public funding to find a solution. Interestingly, it also suggested that 'market-entry rewards' be allowed as a form of compensation to pharmaceutical companies that venture into unprofitable drugs.

My colleagues at Wockhardt were also aware of a May 2013 paper in *Nature Review* that drew attention to a bigger worry, namely, the slowing down of the pace of antibiotic discovery. These reports as well as several others that expressed concern at the relative lack of investment in combating antibiotics resistance only reinforced our belief at Wockhardt that we were on the right track.

In May 2016, a study published by the PEW Charitable Trust, a US-based independent non-profit, non-governmental organization, observed that '[...] in recent years, the discovery and development of new antibiotics have slowed dramatically as scientific barriers to drug discovery, regulatory challenges, and diminishing returns on investment have led major drug companies to scale back or abandon their antibiotic research. Consequently, antibiotic discovery—which peaked in the 1970s—has dropped precipitously.'

What is even more startling is that it went on to say, 'Of greater concern is the fact that nearly all antibiotics brought to market over the past 30 years have been variations on existing drugs.' I noted in particular the statement that '[...] every currently available antibiotic is a derivative of a class discovered between the early 1900s and 1984.'

I discussed O'Neill's observations and these reports with Mahesh as we travelled to London in May 2016 to meet Jim O'Neill and apprise him of the work we were doing at Wockhardt. Not only did he seem surprised and happy to learn about our work but he also asked me if the Indian government knew about the kind of R&D we were doing. I did not have a ready answer because we had not briefed the government on our programmes. O'Neill encouraged me to, saying that the Indian government ought to know what was happening in antibiotics research and drug discovery, and also what we were doing in our own way to meet the challenge.

Mahesh and I came away from our meeting with Jim O'Neill satisfied in the knowledge that we were on the right track. In June, we went to Boston to attend the popular American Society for Microbiology's ASM Microbe 2016 conference. As I attended the sessions, I understood why my scientist colleagues were always so excited to attend this conference. It is the go-to place for anybody interested in this area. It is the largest gathering of microbiologists in the world and has been an annual pilgrimage centre for infectious disease scientists and clinical researchers from across the world for several years now. What struck me at the 2016 event were three things: first, the fact that Wockhardt created a world record by exhibiting five new molecules that were in the clinical stage and not in the very early discovery stage. Second, we had made more than fifty scientific poster presentations describing various aspects of the new molecules under development by Wockhardt. Poster presentations are an important means of making presentations at scientific gatherings and enable the announcement of the arrival/birth of a new drug or a clinical candidate in the product pipeline to the scientific and pharma community. And finally, the fact that some of the leading international scientists like David Livermore, an expert clinical microbiologist, and Robert Bonomo, an expert on betalactams, spoke on the interesting features of Wockhardt's new drugs. What could have been better than this at an event where the pharma industry loves to showcase its antiinfective products in their research pipeline by giving glimpses of the new product features.

It was at the end of this conference that I saw the light at the end of that long tunnel of research. Interactions with those in the know in this field at the conference gave us the confidence that we were on to something. Our molecules were now ready to reach the advanced clinical stage of development.

The world is grappling with the problem of bacterial drug resistance against currently known antibiotics. Antimicrobial Resistance (AMR) occurs when microorganisms (such as bacteria, viruses, fungi and parasites) change in ways that render the medications used to cure the infections they cause ineffective. When the microorganisms become resistant to most antimicrobials, they are often referred to as 'superbugs'. These resistant infections are usually associated with higher rates of mortality and extended hospitalization. Both the resistant bacteria and the genes responsible for resistance could spread to other normal bacteria and make them drug resistant, imposing huge costs on individuals and society.

AMR is of particular concern in developing countries like India, as the burden of infectious disease is high and healthcare spending is low. Today, India has one of the highest bacterial disease burdens and the second highest antibiotics consumption in the world. Therefore, to overcome the morbidity and mortality due to these infections, novel antibiotics effective against superbugs have a critical role.

A recently concluded seven-year surveillance study in India, sponsored by the Bill and Melinda Gates Foundation, covering major hospitals and community pantogens from 696 sectors, concluded that antibiotic resistance has become significant in many cases of Klebsiella, Pseudomonas, Acinetobacter, E.coli and S.aureus (MRSA), and ranges from 47 to 80 per cent. These are life-threatening organisms.

It is precisely by battling these that Wockhardt's WCK 5222 and other antibiotics in our drug discovery programme will help control the menace of superbug resistance. Over the last twenty years, Wockhardt has synthesized over 6,000 chemical molecules and now has five drugs that have entered Phase II and Phase III clinical trials. The USFDA has given all these drugs a breakthrough status, that is, the Qualified Infectious Disease Product (QIDP) status. This status holds huge significance and is a path-breaking initiative by the USFDA. It follows a bill in the House of Representatives in the US in June 2011 'to provide incentives for the development of qualified infectious disease products'. It paves the way for accelerated drug development, which really boils down to shorter time spent in clinical trials and there is also an assurance of faster review by the regulator. In other words, drugs with promise stand a good chance of getting quicker approvals by the regulator.

Three of these drugs are for gram positive organisms and two of these drugs are for gram negative organisms. Over the last ten years, global patents filed for antibiotics have declined by 60 per cent, whereas patents filed by Wockhardt in these ten years have increased by 315 per cent. There are ten other companies that are involved in antibiotic research and collectively have eleven drugs in the pipeline at the clinical stage. However, Wockhardt alone has five drugs.

In early 2017, the Wockhardt research team had a meeting with the USFDA's New Drug Antibiotic Regulatory team at which the USFDA agreed to an abridged clinical trial for Phase III for Wockhardt's super drug antibiotic WCK 5222. This was based on the evaluation by the USFDA of the pre-clinical and clinical data from Phase I, establishing the safety and clinical scope of the efficacy of the drug. WCK 5222 contains zidebactam, developed by Wockhardt's drug discovery team.

WCK 5222 is a super drug that introduces an entire new class of antibiotic treatment. It meets the urgent threat of Carbopenem-resistant Enterobacteriaceae and serious threats like multidrug-resistant Acinetobacter, extended spectrum β-lactamase (ESBLs) producing Enterobacteriaceae, drug-resistant Salmonella typhi and multidrug-resistant Pseudomonas aeruginosa. This is the categorization based on which the USFDA has given WCK 5222 the special QIDP status.

Wockhardt has taken this antibiotic for worldwide clinical development.

Thus, WCK 5222 is expected to be a life-saving destination therapy for serious hospital-acquired infections such as pneumonia, ventilator-associated pneumonia and bloodstream infections. At Wockhardt we believe that on the successful clinical outcome of super drug WCK 5222, millions of lives will be saved. Wockhardt expects global clinical launch of WCK 5222 during the year 2020–21.

∽

At the end of a long journey, we have arrived where we are today. Wockhardt is the only pharmaceutical company in the world to have five experimental antibiotic drugs that have been granted the QIDP status by the USFDA. My grandchildren used to put up their hands and say, 'Give me a high five'. That's what our drug discovery programme has done.

Today, I am happy that not only did we measure our risks well, but also chose the right way forward. Of course, being in business requires a spirit of adventure and enterprise. The great economist John Maynard Keynes called it 'animal spirits'. The urge to hunt and kill. But every successful business knows that one must also get a measure of the risks involved.

The secret to success in research is no different from the secret of success in business. One sees what everyone sees. But, one must imagine what no one else does. It is all in the mind. I have always been inspired by John Kennedy's declaration in 1961 that the United States would put a man on the moon. By summer 1969, the US fulfilled Kennedy's dream. Recently, Prime Minister Narendra Modi gave an inspiring call for the building of a 'New India'. It is a vision that inspires us at Wockhardt. We too have dreamed big. We have gathered innovative minds. Their imagination has brought us to where we are: on the threshold of new drug discovery. We have made a commitment to humanity that with our drug discovery programme, we will save millions of lives worldwide.

*Habil Khorakiwala greeting Prime Minister Narendra Modi*
*at the US–India Business Council meeting in 2016*

I first met Habil Khorakiwala in 2010 in Boston. I had been asked to take over the international programmes at Partners HealthCare International, a daunting task for an academic cardiologist. A programme from Harvard Medical School had been transitioned to Partners HealthCare International and needed to be integrated with a small programme already in existence; the global downturn of 2008 raised serious issues as to the viability of all these efforts.

I knew the Wockhardt relationship had been critically important to Harvard Medical School and to our future, and was understandably apprehensive when I was asked to meet the company's chairman for lunch at a Boston hotel—my first one-on-one meeting as an international negotiator.

The chairman was small in stature but much larger in presence and purpose than I had imagined. His agenda was simple. He was on a mission to help a relative with an advanced heart disease, and he wanted to know all the nuances, all the options for heart failure management. We touched upon all options, therapies and end-of-life issues. This chairman wanted all the insight to do what was right. He was compassionate, insightful and understood the limitations, promise and the future of medical care.

And I would learn that this is how he approaches medicine. The new hospital in Mumbai was not just an investment; it was to respond to the future of India's healthcare needs with an innovative mission. It was to be a patient-centric and compassionate facility, in line with his personality. To be sure, it would deploy the latest technology, and be equipped to tackle the scourges of diabetes, strokes, cancer and, of course, heart failure. He was not just interested in developing the best clinical programmes, but had the vision to incorporate it with the very best research minds of the Wockhardt enterprise. The long-term future of stem cell transplant was as important to him as disease-management strategies. His pride in the mission of healthcare is reflected by all members of the Wockhardt family.

I will long remember the pride with which the nurses showed me their new information system. Their pleasure at being at the forefront of medical technology was immediately evident. Simply put, professional development was doing the right thing.

Then in summer 2016, I had dinner with the chairman, again in Boston. He was in town for a pharmaceutical industry meeting with many of his colleagues and employees. He readily admitted that he knew little of the science that they were promoting; rather, he took immense personal pride in being part of such a dynamic and innovative workforce.

Habil Khorakiwala and I share the same commitment to family and friends. The warmth, love and admiration that surround him in Mumbai are palpable. His strength is not just his business acumen or his strategic insight; rather, it is his greatness that rests solely in humanism, his commitment to reduce the suffering of mankind, and the pride he takes in sharing this mission with others.

What have I learned from Habil Khorakiwala?

Be true to your values. Be open-minded. Be supportive. And the rest will follow...

**Gilbert H. Mudge**, MD,
President and CEO, Partners HealthCare International;
Professor of Medicine, Harvard Medical School,
Boston, Massachusetts

## Chapter 2

# A Boy from Bombay

*If I have the belief that I can do it, I shall surely acquire the capacity to do it, even if I may not have it at the beginning.*

—Mahatma Gandhi

Bombay is the city that the Khorakiwala family adopted at the turn of the 19th century. My grandfather, Taherbhai Ebrahimji Khorakiwala, migrated to Bombay (Mumbai) in 1896 from Palanpur in the Indian state of Gujarat. He left his large mansion, rented a small apartment in Mumbai and started a kirana shop, a provision store. Mumbai was by then the subcontinent's most important centre of commerce and finance. My grandfather saw his decision to move to Mumbai as an investment in the future. He believed the family would make its mark in Mumbai and that Mumbai would make its mark in the world.

The kirana shop, on Gunbow Street in the Fort area, was named after my grand-uncle. Beginning as the Akbarally Ebrahimji Drug Store, it grew into a multi-product retail shop and was branded as 'Akbarallys'—a simple, smart, easy-to-remember name. In 1955, my father took charge of the store and developed it into more of a department store, even a supermarket. It was a new concept in

Mumbai. One could buy everything from foodstuffs and clothes to electrical goods and pharmaceuticals. New branch stores were opened in different parts of the city. Akbarallys came to represent a new concept in retail trade. The growth of Akbarallys was both on account of the decline and exit of British-owned stores, like Whiteway and Laidlow, Army & Navy Store and Evans and Fraser, and the fact that the brand had come to be identified with good quality. When I look back, I must confess, I am impressed by my father's entrepreneurial courage and acumen. He was not only entering a line of business that many others were exiting, but was also prescient in branding it with a name that every Mumbaikar would come to remember in years to come.

Everyone who migrates is a risk-taker. Equally, he is ambitious, entrepreneurial, creative and willing to work hard. The immigrant entrepreneur works doggedly to succeed in a new place for he has nowhere else to go. His ego prevents him from returning to his home base in case of failure. He has after all left home to find success elsewhere. So he has to succeed. He has to make a mark and not just a living. The desire to succeed in a new place pulls one out of one's comfort zone.

My grandfather was imbued with that sense of purpose and the urge to do something that he would feel proud of. He worked hard and immersed himself wholeheartedly in his business. My father inherited that spirit of enterprise. He was devoted to the assurance of good quality and wanted Akbarallys to be viewed as a one-stop shop of high quality.

When I look back at the last hundred years of our family history, I am convinced that my grandfather would have been proud to see how closely the Khorakiwala family has come to be identified with his adopted city. Even though today's Mumbai has many fancy shops and malls, every Mumbaikar associates the name Akbarallys with this metropolis.

That was the first lesson in building a business that I learnt from my family elders—my grandfather, my father and his siblings—that even as one grows bigger and goes higher, one must always remain rooted in the ground. It is the strength of one's roots that helps one branch out and grow.

∽

I was just about ten when I had my first lesson in biology. Uncle Hussaini, my father's youngest brother, was studying zoology at college. One day, he brought home a frog and invited me to be his audience as he dissected it. A frog's anatomy has much in common with a human being's, he explained to me as he laid the frog on its back and spread and pinned its limbs down on a board. I was a curious and willing audience. He gently lifted its skin with tweezers and made an incision with a scalpel. Slowly but confidently he separated the skin from the muscle and laid bare the inside of the amphibian. I was awestruck.

If my first lessons in biology were learnt from my uncle, I learnt the ropes of business from my father. Fakhruddin Taherbhai Khorakiwala was the head of a joint family. In those times, the head of a large joint family was always a distant figure. My father was more than just the head of a family. He was also a community leader. Many members of our community, the Dawoodi Bohras, visited us at home and my father was always available to them. In the 1950s, he became close to the Syedna, the religious leader of the Dawoodi Bohra community, and organized several programmes to promote liberal values such as modern education and community-based healthcare. Years later, in 1992, he entered public life to become the Sheriff of Mumbai and was then elected to become the president of the Indian Merchants' Chamber.

My father was a disciplinarian, but he and my mother both played their part. If he was strict, she was soft. My mother made sure we held our father in great regard. My father rarely praised his children.

Our mother was the one who spoilt us. She was always anxious about our welfare and worried a lot when we went out to play and did not return home when we were expected to. My uncle Shafaqat was also a disciplinarian. He was very conservative too. He did not like our listening to Hindi film songs on the radio. Like many young people in my generation, I liked listening to Binaca Geetmala on Radio Ceylon. Uncle Shafaqat disapproved of it. If he ever walked into the house when we were listening to film music, he would promptly switch the radio off.

My father was born to be an entrepreneur, always willing to take a risk and do something new. As a young man of twenty-two, he left Mumbai to try his hand at business in Calcutta (now Kolkata), a new place. He discovered that a ship coming from Southeast Asia was bringing in a cargo of candy. He found a financier in Kolkata who agreed to lend him the money to buy the consignment. However, those were the war years, the early 1940s. He was unable to sell the stock as quickly as he had hoped to. It took him over three years to get rid of the candy and return home. It was a learning experience and one that did not discourage him from exploring new opportunities in the years to come.

As I grew up, I became very proud of my father because I began to recognize the values he upheld in business. He would never do business with a friend because he did not want differences in business to spoil a friendship. Like my grandfather, he too would always emphasize the importance of fairness in business. 'Never cheat a customer,' he would always say. That principle has remained with me through life. Play fair— in business, in relationships, in whatever one does. Our family business exemplified that. I recall Akbarallys never had differential pricing even in the days when customers were used to bargaining. Long before the government introduced the concept of fixed price and maximum retail price (MRP), Akbarallys introduced the concept of fixed price, which included all taxes. No fudging there. The customer knew the exact and final price of what she was buying. Fairness required transparency.

My father was actively involved in the Council for Fair Business Practices (CFBP), becoming its chairman. The Council was established on Gandhi Jayanti—2 October 1966. Some of the other members of the Council were J.R.D. Tata, Ramakrishna Bajaj, Arvind Mafatlal, Naval Tata, S.P. Godrej, J.N. Guzder, Ashok Birla, B.D. Garware, D.M. Khatau, Harish Mahindra and Vishnubhai Haribhakti.

My father was truly committed to the idea of fair business practice and inculcated that spirit in me. The learning I acquired at my father's feet has played an important part in shaping my being, my personality and my character. It was not just his spoken words that guided me but, more importantly, his unspoken ones. I observed his actions, his acts of omission and commission and drew my own lessons from them.

*The Khorakiwala family*

While my father remained rooted in the world of Mumbai business, his itch to travel never left him and he would often go on long trips, sometimes taking my mother with him. He loved travelling and was entrepreneurial even in his travels, going to places off the beaten track and exploring new destinations. Years later at a picnic party organized by his colleagues and staff they presented him with a globe and one of them took out a pen and asked my father to tick all the places around the world that he had been to. I was truly in awe when I discovered he had visited every continent, with dozens of tick marks around the globe.

When I was around twelve, my father decided that we children would also accompany him on a holiday. It was not just an ordinary holiday. The entire family, including our grandfather, set off on a holiday-cum-pilgrimage to holy places in the Middle East. My father decided to get a suit stitched for me to take on the trip since there would be occasions when I would have to be dressed properly and formally. A grey pinstriped suit was tailored for me and I preened in front of a mirror as any young man would, after wearing it.

We set sail from Mumbai on a cruise liner and crossed the Arabian Sea and up the Suez Canal to Egypt, Jordan, Iraq and, what was then still, Palestine. We visited holy places in Jerusalem and Iraq, and historic and ancient sites in Egypt and Jordan. Finally, we sailed to the beautiful island of Cyprus. It was the most exciting trip I had ever made.

My real bonding with my father had to wait till I left home to attend college in Ahmedabad. Absence makes the heart grow fonder. I began to miss home and my parents and looked forward to holidays. What surprised me was that my father too seemed to miss me. He would always make it a point to come to the railway station to receive me when I came home from the hostel.

It was around that time that I recall writing to him, admitting to having made some mistake. I have never forgotten his response.

'It requires courage to recognize that one has made a mistake,' he wrote back. 'It requires even greater courage to admit it.'

Those words have stayed with me. As a father and as Chairman of Wockhardt, I cannot recall ever penalizing someone for making an honest mistake. I believe there is nothing wrong in making a mistake as long as one does not repeat it. That shows an unwillingness to learn and rectify. People and companies grow only by making mistakes, recognizing them, admitting the mistakes and learning from them.

The Mumbai of my childhood and youth was a nice place to grow up in. Ours was a middle-class family and our pleasures were very simple. The high point of fun was going to the beach for ice cream and joining members of our family and the staff of our family shop, Akbarallys, on an occasional picnic.

My schooling was at Bharda New High School in the Fort area. I was a diligent student, but I was also interested in sports. We would go to Azad Maidan to play cricket. After entering high school another favourite pastime was going to the cinema, and I would often go with my friends. Our favourite cinema house for English movies was New Empire, while we saw Hindi movies at Capital cinema near VT station. My favourite actress was Madhubala and my favourite actor was Dilip Kumar.

An event that remains etched in my memory from my childhood is Gandhiji's assassination. I was barely six years old at the time. Everyone at home heard the news in utter shock and silence. It was clear even to a child like me that something catastrophic had happened. Apart from the sadness that enveloped the household, a palpable sense of fear gripped the elders. It was the kind of fear that we would experience years later, in late December 1992 and January 1993, when communal riots broke out across the city. My father was the Sheriff of Mumbai at the time.

As we remained gripped by fear, our entire family was protected from attackers by our Hindu neighbours. We were living in Maker Towers at the time. Our neighbours removed all the nameplates so that no one could identify the residents by their religion. They steadfastly refused entry to any outsiders till the police arrived and order was restored. My father later organized a ten-kilometre-long human chain including people of all faiths as an expression of unity and solidarity against divisive and communal forces.

For me, it was an experience that I would never forget. I was stuck in New Delhi for a couple of days and was finally able to take a late night flight back to Mumbai. My father drove to the airport to escort me back home. As the Sheriff of Mumbai, he had police protection. Unfortunately, my flight was inordinately delayed, and I wasn't able to let my father know as in those days it was not easy to make telephone calls to other cities. The era of mobile telephony had not yet dawned in India. Having waited at the airport in vain, he returned home. My flight finally landed in Mumbai at some unearthly hour. As I entered the terminal, I found no one there to meet me. I was not sure if it would be safe for me to take a taxi home, or if I would even be able to get a taxi at that hour. Luckily, I met a fellow Rotarian, Virendra Bhat, who had come to the airport to see off a guest. When he realized that I was stranded, he offered to drop me home in his car. Sitting huddled in the car in complete silence, we drove through an eerily deserted Mumbai. Every now and then, we would see small groups of people. And along the way, we often saw something or the other burning—vehicles, shops, or just rubbish. Fear enveloped me. It was a terrifying experience, but one that brought us closer to our friends and neighbours. The spirit of Mumbai shone brightly even in that dark hour.

∽

It was 1959 and I was seventeen years old. School was done; I had to decide what I would do next. Uncle Hussaini encouraged me to study pharmacy. By then our family business had also entered that field. My father had just bought into a chemical company, Worli Chemical Works. So he supported my decision to seek a bachelor's degree in pharmacy. He was happy that I had chosen to enter this line of business. I enrolled myself in the L.M. College of Pharmacy in Ahmedabad. Set up by the well-known Ahmedabad Education Society in 1947, the college received its initial endowment from Seth Lallubhai Motilal, hence its name. It was reputed to be one of the best colleges for pharmacy. There was only one problem. I had to leave home and move to Ahmedabad.

Moving from the hustle and bustle of Mumbai and its big city life to the relatively humdrum life of Ahmedabad was in itself a difficult transition. But more daunting was the transition from the comforts of home to hostel life.

The pharmacy course was easy to handle. But hostel life was marred by the fact that they served us only vegetarian fare. I think every child who complains about the food at home should go through the experience of hostel life. Every weekend, I would travel a good fifteen to twenty kilometres, a long distance in those days of slower travel, to visit my uncle and tuck into good Bohra non-vegetarian cuisine.

After two years of hostel life and seeing me travel every weekend to his house for home-cooked food, my uncle took pity on me and invited me to live with him. My father was equally generous. He gifted me a Lambretta scooter to enable me to journey to college. The B. Pharma course is a five-year graduate programme. For the next three years, I was the proud owner of a two-wheeler at college. It was a big deal in those days.

I graduated in 1964. The big news that summer was the passing away of Prime Minister Jawaharlal Nehru. There was considerable gloom at home. Nehru had become a household name across India, having been the country's first prime minister and in office for a continuous period of seventeen years.

I busied myself planning for the future and it was finally decided that I should seek a master's degree in pharmacy from a good institution in the United States. Although my father encouraged me to go to the US, my mother was most unhappy. I would be the first in our entire family to go abroad for higher education. She did not see the point of it. Not only would she miss me, but she worried that I might go astray in a distant land with an alien culture.

Perhaps my father worried too. He decided to take me on a pilgrimage to important holy shrines of the Dawoodi Bohra Muslims. We visited our holy shrines at Burhanpur in Madhya Pradesh, and at Surat, Godhra and Ahmedabad in Gujarat. At that time, I only viewed it as a pilgrimage, a two-week religious tour meant to vaccinate me against alien cultural influences. But later in life, I recognized that the trip gave me an opportunity to bond with my father. Our relationship was secured during those travels.

But my parents were not yet adequately reassured that their son could now set sail; they wanted me to spend some time with the Syedna. Called the Da'I al-Mutlaq, the Syedna is the revered religious leader of the Dawoodi Bohras. Syedna Taher Saifuddin, the fifty-first Syedna, knew our family well. My father arranged for me to meet him. It was well known that the Syedna stayed up late into the night. So I was not surprised to be told that he would meet me at 11 p.m. on the appointed day.

On reaching his place, I was asked to wait outside till I was summoned. The night proceeded at its own pace as I sat there waiting to be called. It was 2 a.m., when the Syedna finally called me in. He was seated in a sparsely furnished room. There were just the two of us. He asked me what I had done, how I spent my time and about my plans. He then spoke at length about India and Islam.

I could see he wanted me to remember everything he was saying. He wanted this interaction to be etched in my mind so that even when I was away in the US, in a distant foreign land, I would always remember what he had said. He did not want me to lose my connect with home, with our family values, with my religion and my country. As I returned home in the early hours of a new day, I knew that my university in the US would only be a way station in the journey of life. That my destiny was back home, here in Mumbai.

The visits to holy shrines in India and the meeting with the Syedna were not the only preparation of the soil with which my father wanted to ensure I remained rooted in our culture. He ensured that the itinerary of my travel to the US included a visit to Karbala, in Iraq. Karbala is among the great holy places in Islam, being home to the shrine of Imam Hussain, a grandson of Prophet Mohammed. In those days, most flights to the US from Mumbai would make refuelling halts along the way and one such stop was Beirut. I interrupted my journey in Beirut and travelled to Karbala. Beirut was a lively city—a 'Paris of the Middle East'—and Baghdad was a great centre of knowledge and learning. The destruction of these cities, of their life and lifestyles, of the great libraries and centres of learning, is one of the greatest tragedies of the past half century.

Returning to Beirut, I boarded the flight that would finally take me to the West. To Europe and then the US. A part of the world that in the years to come would emerge as the main market for what my endeavours at Wockhardt would create.

༄

In the fall of 1964, I was admitted to a Master of Science course in pharmacy at Purdue University at Indianapolis. I adjusted quite easily to hostel life, having lived that life in India. I also settled into my studies fairly quickly. I made friends, a few of whom liked the good life and devoted a lot of time to their hobbies and other non-academic pursuits. One of my class fellows spent all his free time playing golf, another was obsessed with cars and bought himself a Studebaker. I got along well with my friends, but my focus, as indeed that of most of my fellow Indians on campus, remained on academics.

In my second year, I made friends with a student, Narendra Bansilal. He later returned home to take up a government job. Narendra was a good cook and would cook spicy Indian non-vegetarian food. We decided to rent an apartment and live in this shared accommodation. For me, it was a win–win situation, since he did most of the cooking!

Purdue had the practice of professors inviting students home for informal conversations. The first time I was invited, my professor told me to be at his home by seven in the evening. Being the Indian I was and given our usual dinner time, I assumed the invitation was for dinner. To my dismay, I discovered on arrival that the professor, like most Americans, had finished his supper and was ready to offer a drink as we sat down for a chat.

My course had several Indians. Most of them stayed back in the US. Only a handful of us from the Class of 1966, such as Ajit Shirodkar and Jayakumar Shah, a senior, returned home. Our friendship has been a great reward for me and I feel happy that many of us have remained in touch over the years.

I was all of twenty-four when I completed my master's programme at Purdue and returned home. As soon as I got back, I immersed myself in work, joining my father's company, Worli Chemical Works. I knew that this was not what I was going to do for the rest of my life. I was clear in my mind that I had to strike out on my own and get involved in something new. But Worli Chemical Works provided a good training ground. My father and a business partner of his had acquired and run the company for nearly a decade. By 1964, it was on the verge of closure. We managed to turn it around.

∽

*Habil Khorakiwala after being conferred an honorary doctorate by Purdue University. He is the first non-American in the 125-year history of College of Pharmacy, Purdue University, to receive this unique honour. Left to right: President of Purdue University, France A. Cordova; Habil Khorakiwala; Nafisa Khorakiwala; and dean of College of Pharmacy, Purdue University, Craig K. Svensson*

Even as I maintained a regular work schedule, I began reconnecting with old friends. Through my friends, I met a young college student who was studying at St Xavier's in Mumbai. We struck up a conversation and, as the stories go, one thing led to another. I was by then twenty-six, but Nafisa was just twenty when I proposed to her. My parents had been scouting around for alliances for me, but I gathered the courage to tell them that I had found someone for myself. Parents on both sides had to meet and approve of our choice. We went through the accepted traditional norms of confirming the alliance and an engagement. Nafisa had to complete her graduation. We got engaged in 1967 and our wedding was fixed for 26 May 1969, precisely two weeks after her final examinations.

*Habil Khorakiwala and wife Nafisa on their wedding day. Alongside are both sets of parents: Fakhruddin T. Khorakiwala and Khadija F. Khorakiwala (front row); and Nafisa's parents Haiderbhai Latif and Sugrabai Latif (back row)*

We lived a surprisingly ordered life during our first year of marriage. Weekdays were all about work, Saturdays were ours—Nafisa's and mine, and we would invariably go for a movie and eat out every Saturday—and Sundays were spent with the family. In November 1970, our firstborn, Huzaifa, arrived. In September 1972 Murtaza was born. It was only after a decade, on 16 September 1982, that our daughter Zahabiya arrived. Our children were the joy of our lives. But, for me, those were also years of intense business and social activity.

At work, we were taking important decisions. In 1973, our family firm, Worli Chemical Works, made way for the newly registered Wockhardt Private Limited. We decided to manufacture and market pharmaceuticals. The year before, in 1972, we had had to begin the process of finding a new home for our manufacturing facilities since our landlord wanted to repossess the land on which Worli Chemical Works stood. I decided that rather than look for alternative accommodation near Mumbai, we should move to one of the regions that the government was promoting as a destination for new business. That is how we came to move to Aurangabad in 1976. A new phase of my life was about to begin.

As I entered my thirty-fifth year, I knew a new adventure was about to begin. I was confident that I was prepared for it. My family was my first centre of learning. My parents instilled in me the self-confidence to go forth. Positive family bonding helped me imbibe positive values; it defined my personality and my relationship with people. I valued quality and honesty in all walks of life. The mosaic of spirituality I had imbibed early in life, gave me the instinct to care for people and society. In life, it provided balance and enhanced my inner strength and self-belief. It enabled me to maintain inner calm even when surrounded by turmoil.

*Wockhardt was given the first Quality Excellence Award instituted by the Government of India; Habil Khorakiwala receiving this award from former President of India K.R. Narayanan*

I first met Khorakiwala, in 2007, when he came to Purdue to receive our Distinguished Alumnus award. He was well known as one of our most accomplished alumni, and I was delighted to have the opportunity to meet him. I was immediately struck by his warm and engaging personality. It was an honour for us to have a man of such accomplishments among our alumni and yet, he repeatedly expressed how honoured he felt to be recognized in this way by our college. My impression on this first encounter was that Habil was a man of tremendous vision with a deep love for his family and passion for meeting the healthcare needs of his fellow countrymen and beyond.

It was my privilege to receive an invitation to visit Habil, in India, and attend his daughter's wedding. I was overwhelmed to be part of the celebrations, and was received with tremendous warmth by Habil and Nafisa. During the visit, I had the opportunity to visit several units of Wockhardt. I was impressed by the forward-thinking strategy that was evident in their development of pharmaceuticals. I also met patients who had travelled from the US to receive treatment in Mumbai. The training and experience of the medical staff, as well as their patient-focused approach, was unexpected by me. The transparency of the cost of treatment was something unparalleled even in the US. After speaking with several patients, I understood why they chose to travel to Mumbai for treatment.

The high regard in which the staff at Wockhardt held the chairman was evident. These were employees who were deeply committed to the mission of the organization and had tremendous confidence in his leadership. To instill that type of perspective in your employees says a lot about one's leadership abilities. I have had the opportunity to engage with and visit numerous pharmaceutical companies over the past decade. However, I have never seen such confidence being expressed in the leader of a pharmaceutical company as I experienced during my visit to Wockhardt.

In 2010, Purdue University awarded Khorakiwala an honorary doctorate, the highest award presented by the university. He was the first non-European international recipient of an honorary doctorate from our college. His visit enabled us to renew our acquaintance and solidified my deep respect for his accomplishments. His perspective on the international pharmaceutical industry and opportunities in India, in particular, were very insightful. Through my conversations with him, I also realized that he had a pulse on the national economy of India that extended much beyond pharmaceuticals and healthcare. He was a man who understood what his country needed to do to continue to advance the economic well-being of its citizens.

Over the years, I have watched his various interviews and have always gained important insights into economics, pharmaceutical development, and strategies for meeting healthcare needs in emerging markets.

Habil and Nafisa have provided generous support to our college. Their gifts have enabled us to: support students undertaking summer research experiences in faculty laboratories; develop a new pharmaceutical manufacturing laboratory in our college that is an essential component of our undergraduate and graduate programmes; and providing support for faculty research. Through their generosity, they are helping to prepare another generation of pharmaceutical scientists.

I regret that my travel limitations have prohibited me from having the opportunity to visit Habil in India, in recent years. I consider his friendship and my opportunity to interact with him, to be among the most important highlights of my tenure as dean at the College of Pharmacy, Purdue University. As we mark his 75th birthday and the 50th anniversary of Wockhardt, it is most fitting to acknowledge the remarkable impact he has had for his extensive career. We are incredibly proud to acknowledge him as an alumnus of our institution!

**Craig K. Svensson**, dean of College of Pharmacy,
Purdue University, USA

Chapter 3

# From Worli to the World

*To sustain and conduct successful business, one requires learning the in-depth requisites and tactics of modern business; diversify and expand accordingly; and take advantage of technology and science.*

—Syedna Mohammed Burhanuddin

The 1970s began on a historic note for Indian business. The Government of India, under Indira Gandhi's new leadership, was redefining the country's economic landscape. It was a mixed bag of disruptive and supportive interventions. In 1969 several private commercial banks were nationalized with a view to improving credit availability for the farming and other 'priority' sectors. In the same year, the Monopolies and Restrictive Trade Practices Act was enacted, imposing new curbs on big business houses. The already restrictive industrial licensing policy was further amended in 1970, imposing new restrictions on foreign as well as Indian firms, including keeping big business out of several areas of manufacturing that were reserved for small businesses. Much of this was resented by domestic business, even though it gave Indira Gandhi a new political profile.

However, there were a series of important policy interventions made by the government in 1970 pertaining to the drugs and pharmaceutical industry that we in the industry generally welcomed, even though they too were a mixed bag. The policy initiatives included: (a) the enactment of the Indian Patents Act, 1970, which came into effect with its notification in April 1972; till then, patents in India had been governed by the archaic Patents and Designs Act of 1911; (b) the notification of a Drugs Price Control Order in 1970; and (c) the setting up of a government Committee on Drugs and Pharmaceutical (Hathi Committee) that was asked to define a policy framework aimed at facilitating the growth of an indigenous drugs and pharmaceutical industry and promoting domestic research, while ensuring the availability of affordable medicines.

The two important provisions of the Patents Act that defined the policy framework for the pharmaceutical industry were: (a) patents would be granted only for processes, not products; and (b) automatic licences could be issued three years after the granting of the patent. The Act also defined the time frame for a patent as five years from the date of a patent being granted or seven years from the date of application, whichever was less. While there were several inadequacies in the new regime, the new patent law gave a boost to domestic manufacturing of drugs and pharmaceuticals.

It was clear to me that we had to adopt a more aggressive approach to growing our business given the opportunity being provided. India had a large number of pharmaceutical firms by then, but mostly in the unregulated small-scale sector. Almost 90 per cent of the total capacity in the sector was in small-scale plants. There were a large number of foreign companies and a few Indian ones. The production of drugs and pharmaceuticals in 1970 totalled up to no more than $600 million. Of this, a fifth was in bulk drugs and the rest in formulations.

I knew this structure of production and sales would not last for too long. We were at the cusp of change and Wockhardt had to ride the new wave. Our first step was to change the definition of our business by converting our family firm, Worli Chemical Works, into a partnership firm, Wockhardt Pharmaceuticals. The name was derived from a mix of letters from the words 'Worli' and 'chemicals' and made to sound like a German name! In 1973, within a year of the notification of the Patents Act, the partnership firm was registered as Wockhardt Private Limited. As we began to focus more on pharmaceuticals and bulk drugs I realized that our premises in Worli were becoming increasingly restrictive in terms of space, and the opportunity cost of being located in Mumbai was going up.

It was around that time that the state government of Maharashtra introduced backward area development incentives for firms locating away from urban centres and setting up factories in less developed regions of the state. I found Aurangabad to be an attractive centre for setting up a pharmaceutical facility. But before I could even think about how I would raise the funds and organize the effort, I had to first contend with the reaction of my family and community elders.

For my father, Mumbai was a zone of comfort. He was not enthusiastic about locating facilities too far away from it. Moreover, as he reminded me, ours was a Muslim business family and we had the support system of family, friends and the larger Dawoodi Bohra community in Mumbai. It was a safe territory to function in. Could a young Muslim entrepreneur like me function in a semi-urban area like Aurangabad, with all the local political pulls and pressures? My father was against the move.

Once again, he roped in our community elders. He would urge each one of them to advise me against moving out of Mumbai. All this put me in a quandary. Was I being foolish? Foolhardy? Risking the business that my father had nurtured and built for the sake of some future growth and expansion? Should I stay put in Mumbai and limit our operations and my ambitions?

It was a period of tremendous self-doubt and I strived hard to overcome the fear inside me. For months I agonized and for months the discussion went on. Every now and then my father would introduce me to someone who would advise me against the move. Out of that self-doubt, out of the agony of that internal debate within myself, out of that conflict between the urge to be entrepreneurial and the pressure to play it safe, I finally emerged having decided that I would venture forth.

How long would I live in fear? How long would I allow others to make me live in fear? Was the choice between living in safety and comfort and dying every day living in fear? I urged my father to allow me to invest and seek growth in Aurangabad. He finally relented.

⨍

Why Aurangabad? Several state governments were offering backward area development incentives including tax holidays, interest rate subvention and so on and identifying new locations within each state for the localization of manufacturing activity in less developed regions. I chose to restrict my search to Maharashtra and Gujarat and, after visiting several places, opted for Aurangabad. It was a city unlike most other centres located near district towns. It had an airport and good hotels, thanks to it being an important tourist destination.

The city also had forward-looking political leadership, in particular the late Rafiq Zakaria, a Member of Parliament (MP), a senior leader of the Indian National Congress party and the father of the American media personality Fareed Zakaria. The elder Zakaria had played an active role in the creation and development of the industrial estate in Aurangabad. His presence there gave me the confidence to make the move. We set up what later went on to be India's first USFDA-approved formulations making unit in the industrial zone of Chikalthana—also the first of the twelve Wockhardt manufacturing units. We refer to this facility as L1—the unit for manufacturing formulations.

Ours was the first pharmaceutical manufacturing facility in

Aurangabad. Today, it is home to over a dozen companies. The Indian pharmaceutical industry is largely localized in Andhra Pradesh, Gujarat and Maharashtra and almost all major firms, with a few exceptions, are based in these three states. Maharashtra became my karmabhoomi.

Once my decision to set up base in Aurangabad was approved by my family, I became fully involved in its execution. I approached Professor S.K. Chatterjee, a professor in the pharmacy department at Bombay University, who I knew had specialized in conceptualizing designs for modern pharmaceutical manufacturing facilities. I had great regard for his skill and invited him to design our new facility. His design was of course based on the concept of flow of material. But what impressed me about him was his vision. He had laid out clearly how a given shop floor could be expanded with growth over a period of time without any changes to the basic structure. It is a testimony to his vision and conceptualization that we have not had to make any changes to our L1 facility in Aurangabad, which he had designed for us almost four decades back, even though that facility's production capacity and range has hugely expanded. That was the first lesson I learnt in industrial design.

My cousin Juzer took charge of the facility's construction, supervising every detail and making the facility fully operational. It was a great learning opportunity for him. I would visit Aurangabad often to oversee the execution of the project. In those days there was only one big hotel in the city, Rama International, and I would always stay there. Aurangabad was still a small town and it was only during the tourist season that the hotel would be filled with visitors to the nearby historic Ajanta and Ellora cave temples. On one visit I found the entire hotel staff paying very special attention to me. When I asked them why I was getting such singular attention, I was told that I was the only guest staying there at the time!

Given the frequency of my visits I became friends with the hotel's very enterprising and charming general manager, Habib Rehman.

Major Rehman, as I recall him, was a Hyderabadi, had entered the hospitality business after retirement from the army, and took a keen interest in what was cooked for me. We became good friends. It was the combination of his skills in hospitality and management and his tremendous personal charm and elegance that attracted the attention of ITC's senior managers, who snatched him away and later inducted him into their board. Habib is the creator of many of ITC's world-class restaurants, including the iconic Bukhara and Dum Pukht.

Along with the move to Aurangabad I initiated a series of innovations. Till the early 1970s, most drug companies marketed their products through medical representatives who were given printed leaflets providing information on the products being sold. I found that a lot of the printed material would get wasted. So, I introduced visual aids that gave doctors a better appreciation of the drugs being sold, while at the same time reducing the cost of marketing. Those were still early days as far as the use of information technology (IT) was concerned. But we were able to create visual aids that medical representatives could use repeatedly while making their presentations to doctors. Apart from saving cost, there was also a certain novelty attached to the use of new technology in marketing that grabbed a doctor's attention. All this has now become common industry practice.

My next move was to enter into the nutrition business. No pharma company had till then entered this segment of the food industry. There were companies in the nutrition business and there were companies in the pharma business. I viewed both as being part of a common healthcare products industry. Baby food was both nutrition and healthcare. We launched a baby food brand, Dexolac, and then we bought a popular brand, Farex, from Glaxo. Marketing baby foods also gave us experience in the marketing of branded products. But I would always insist that we adhere to a strictly ethical route in the marketing of baby foods.

Once we had established our pharmaceutical facility in Aurangabad, it became clear to me that future growth would have to be based on in-house R&D and that we had to invest in biotechnology. I had come to learn that the United Nations Industrial Development Organization (UNIDO) was funding industrial R&D in the pharmaceutical sector and had supported a research centre in Italy. I put in a bid to establish a joint venture that would enable us to create a biotech research facility in Aurangabad. Wockhardt was the first Indian private sector company to enter into a strategic alliance with UNIDO and secure support for its R&D plans.

The agreement entailed our providing financial support to the New Delhi-based International Centre for Genetic Engineering and Biotechnology (ICGEB). I met K.K. Tiwari, the head of the centre, which was located on the campus of the Jawaharlal Nehru University, and we agreed to develop with him a few biotech products like insulin, hepatitis B vaccine and erythropoietin.

I was aware that investment in R&D required patience. One had to be a long-distance runner. There had to be a singleness of purpose and pursuit. We struggled for three to four years with no initial results. It was then that we brought in Maharaj Kishen Sahib, a molecular biologist who had worked at National Institutes of Health in the US and was then at the Central Drug Research Institute in Lucknow, as the head of our biotechnology research centre. We were the pioneers in the biotechnology space. Other Indian companies started investing in this area only from the late 1990s. Wockhardt was the first mover in biotechnology in India, and became the first Asian company and the third in the world to synthesize, manufacture and successfully market recombinant insulin.

∽

The 1980s was a decade of growth. In 1979, the manufacturing facility at Chikalthana in Aurangabad became operational. We registered Wockhardt Synchem Private Limited the same year and in 1983 Wockhardt Hitech Laboratories Private Limited was incorporated. Wockhardt Synchem manufactured bulk drugs at a new facility at Ankleshwar in Gujarat, while Wockhardt Hitech had a facility at Kalol in Gujarat where we manufactured nutritive foods. The next major milestone in the evolution of our company was the amalgamation of all our facilities under the umbrella of Wockhardt Limited, which was to begin with a closely held public limited company. The decade ended with the setting up of an ultra-modern pharmaceutical facility and a world standard IV fluids manufacturing facility at Waluj, near Aurangabad.

In 1989, we also diversified into the medical services business with a day care OPD centre in Kolkata. This was followed by the opening up of a superspeciality hospital in Bangalore (now Bengaluru), the Wockhardt Hospital and Heart Institute, in 1990. By the time we were ready to go in for an Initial Public Offering (IPO) we had also incorporated a wholly owned subsidiary, Wockhardt International Limited, which dealt with the import and export of pharmaceutical products.

By the mid-1990s, our neighbour, the Ramona moped plant, was shutting down. This opened up an opportunity. I decided to buy the space and converted the moped shed into what became Wockhardt's full-fledged R&D unit. The focus initially was on formulation development and chemical research. From a small research team of about ten people in the early 1990s, that team has grown to be an impressive 650 scientists strong. With colleagues like Mahesh Patel and Maharaj Kishen Sahib heading our R&D facilities, I was confident that we had a fighting chance to make an impact.

❦

*Habil Khorakiwala welcoming the former Chief Minister of Maharashtra, the late Vilasrao Deshmukh, at the inauguration of 'Benchmark—Wockhardt Learning Academy' in the industrial hub of Aurangabad. Also seen is former Maharashtra minister Rajendra Darda. The Academy has classrooms, residential accommodation, a restaurant and complete sports facilities.*

At work, the 1980s was a decade of great stress. At home, it was a decade when my children were making their career decisions. Huzaifa and Murtaza were young men who had by then begun to make their own choices. Huzaifa opted for a degree in commerce while Murtaza decided to study medicine. Zahabiya was still in school. While I spent a considerable amount of time in Aurangabad, Nafisa held the fort at home in Mumbai. I would try and spend my weekends with Nafisa and the children and our favourite weekend activity remained going to the beach for picnics.

*In the Caribbean:*
*Habil Khorakiwala with Murtaza, Huzaifa and Zahabiya*

Even as we celebrated Wockhardt's growth and diversification within the span of a decade, little did we realize that the 1990s would be an even more challenging and exciting decade. The decade began with a bang when the government of Prime Minister P.V. Narasimha Rao introduced radical new economic reforms that not only made it easier to do business in India but also opened up the world for us.

On 24 July 1991, Finance Minister Manmohan Singh was to deliver his first budget speech in Parliament. There was much expectation in the air about changes to fiscal and economic policy. I had kept myself free that evening to listen to the budget speech, but was not prepared to believe the news of the morning. Around noon that day the junior minister for industries held a press conference and announced that the government had decided to do away with what many had come to call the 'Licence-Permit-Quota Raj'. Though the existing system of licensing was not done away with for the drugs and pharmaceutical industry, the overall impact of the industrial liberalization policy was that it boosted investor sentiment and raised confidence in the Indian economy. In the months to come the Narasimha Rao government would also change India's long-standing position on intellectual property rights protection and would sign the Uruguay Round multilateral trade agreement.

The impending intellectual property rights regime would change the game for us in the way we did our business, but the liberalization of the financial markets and the boost to investor sentiment meant that we could raise new funds for research and capacity expansion. Many big companies in Mumbai were looking at raising capital and venturing forth. The new policy also made it easier to bring in foreign investment and created new incentives for promoting exports. Taken together, the industrial and financial markets policy initiatives opened up new possibilities for Indian business and we took advantage of that opportunity.

In April 1992, the government enacted the Securities and Exchange Board of India Act (SEBI Act) with the objective of protecting the interests of investors in securities and to promote the development of and regulate the market for securities. This gave a tremendous boost to investor confidence in the stock market. Several companies took advantage of this new mood of optimism and public confidence to raise funds through public offer of shares. At Wockhardt we had to take a strategic decision. We were still a closely held public limited company and had never tested our appeal to the average investor in the market.

In November 1992, we decided to take that next step with our maiden public issue of shares. We announced a public issue of 3,000,000 equity shares of ₹10 each, for cash, at a premium of ₹185 per share. We had hoped to raise about ₹580 million. Our prospectus drew attention to some of our key strengths: the in-house R&D under way and the recognition it had already received at home and abroad, and the USFDA approvals we had secured. Over half of our production of bulk drugs was being exported and we had emerged as the world's third largest producer of dextropropoxyphene, an analgesic, exporting 68 per cent of our output. Growing annually at the rate of 25 per cent over the previous five years, we were able to attract attention with our offer.

The first public issue turned out to be more dramatic and memorable than we had imagined. It was managed by DSP Merrill Lynch who was the underwriter to the public issue. DSP's Hemendra Kothari felt the reserve price I had set for the issue was too high. I was insistent. I knew my company well and was confident we would be able to convince the market. The issue opened on Thursday, 3 December 1992. DSP had recommended that the issue be kept open till 8 December, as it is normal to keep it open for four working days. My view was different. I knew that the Babri Masjid issue would come up on Sunday, 6 December. Several Hindu leaders had long alleged that the Babri Masjid, erected centuries ago, during Mughal rule, had been built after demolishing a pre-existing Hindu temple. They were demanding that the mosque, or 'disputed structure' as some called it, be brought down and a temple erected. The date fixed for this action was Sunday, 6 December 1992. It was not clear how the political and law and order situation would develop after that and how that would impact the markets in Mumbai. So I suggested that we close the issue early, keeping it open for only two days, till 4 December.

By the end of the first day, the response was very encouraging. Over the next two days, investors picked up the stock and by the end of trade on Saturday, 5 December, we were oversubscribed by four times. We had managed to raise almost ₹675 million, while aiming for ₹580 million. We needed the funds to build our new headquarters in Mumbai's Bandra–Kurla Complex, to expand our facilities in Aurangabad and to invest in research. The market response exceeded our expectations. By that afternoon, we had to take a call. Should we keep the books open or call it a day?

*Habil Khorakiwala with his long-time friend and former Union Minister and former Chief Minister of Jammu & Kashmir, Farooq Abdullah, at the ultra-modern and environment-friendly Wockhardt Tower at the Bandra–Kurla Complex, Mumbai. Also seen is Huzaifa Khorakiwala.*

The reason why this became such an important decision was that the media had started reporting that more than the expected number of what were called 'kar sevaks' had gathered in and around the town of Ayodhya in Uttar Pradesh with the intent to demolish the Babri Masjid and build a temple in its place. In early November, when we took the decision to open our issue on 3 December, no one had imagined that we would be doing so on the eve of a major event in contemporary Indian political and social life. By 5 December, we knew what was happening. Some of my advisers, enthused by the investor response, wanted to keep the issue open for a few more days. Others advised caution. If things went wrong on Sunday, market sentiment would dip on Monday. Nothing would be gained. Even then we had not imagined that the stock market would close down and go into a tailspin.

I had to take a call. I did. I was satisfied with the sum we had raised. Life had already taught me not to be greedy and to be thankful for the good that had come our way. We were oversubscribed several times more than what I had anticipated. We were, after all, the first pharma company in India to go in for a public issue after the liberalization in 1991. The experience was new and the decisions we had to take would have to be based on our own judgement. There was no one else's experience to judge our performance by.

I decided that we had raised the funds we needed. In fact, more than that. It was time to thank the investor and go home. By the end of the working day on 5 December we did precisely that. On 6 December, the Babri Masjid was demolished. On 7 December, the markets collapsed.

❧

The success of the 1992 IPO and the momentum of development that the economic liberalization and reforms of 1991–92 had generated enthused me to cast our net wider. Wockhardt's exports had grown and our financial performance was robust. Between June 1989 and June 1993 Wockhardt's income had risen by 187 per cent and profits before tax had grown by 385 per cent. We were on a roll. Our plans to continue to invest in R&D would make sense only if these could be sustained by revenues at home and abroad. I understood the intricate link between growth and research. Without growth, investment in research would be difficult to sustain. Without research, growth into new products and markets would be difficult.

But to finance both growth and research, we needed funds and global branding. The public issue at home, in 1992, gave us access to funds. That success instilled in me a desire to succeed in a new place, moving outside the comfort zone of the existing business environment. That was also the time that the countries of the EU were integrating into a single market. If one acquired a European presence, one could market across the continent. In January 1994 we incorporated Wockhardt Europe as a wholly owned subsidiary tasked to develop the European market for exports. In February 1994, a month after Wockhardt Europe was incorporated, we announced our decision to raise funds in the global market.

The foray into the global capital market was actually triggered by a visitor from BZW, the investment banking arm of Barclays. This was a few months after the announcement of economic liberalization by Prime Minister Narasimha Rao. Indian companies were allowed to raise funds by way of equity issues in global financial markets. India had begun to attract attention in global capital markets. My visitor from BZW had done his homework and was aware that Indian pharmaceutical companies would attract the attention of global investors. I was not very familiar with the concept of global depository receipts (GDRs) and had till then not thought of them as a source of funds for our global projects. My visitor explained what a GDR was and how he could help me raise funds in a matter of weeks.

I was not yet ready with any specific plans as to how I would use these funds. But I was told that one could raise funds even for a general purpose such as the 'future growth of the company'. Reliance Industries Limited was one of the early birds to raise funds through the issue of GDRs, listing them on the Luxembourg Stock Exchange. Their experience encouraged several major Indian companies to raise capital through GDRs throughout 1993. By the end of 1993, I had done my homework and decided that Wockhardt too should tap this source of funds. I realized that if we could raise foreign equity and fund our research programme as well as our manufacture of exportable medicines, we would be able to acquire a stronger global presence. It would also establish our global credentials.

We offered 2,614,151 GDRs representing an equal number of shares at an issue price of $28.69 per share. Our aim was to raise around $72 million and we ended up raising $75 million. Only a couple of years prior to that we had informally sought a valuation of our shares in a foreign market and the figure I was given was around ₹195 per share. We now received a valuation of ₹900 per share. There was limited dilution of our equity as a result and we raised more than we had hoped to. I took pride in the fact that Wockhardt was the first Indian pharmaceutical company to issue GDRs and list shares on the international market. We were then followed by Ranbaxy and Reddy's.

We informed our potential investors that we were raising these funds to finance our new bulk drugs and IV fluids manufacturing plants as well as a new pesticides plant. We also sought this financing for our rapidly expanding R&D facilities. In seeking to raise funds globally we were also announcing our interest in the global market for drugs and pharmaceuticals. The GDR issue required me to participate in roadshows around the world. Chaperoned by BZW I travelled to London, Edinburgh, Zurich and Hong Kong. In Zurich, I was advised to travel to a meeting with potential investors in a rented Rolls-Royce! One had to step out in style. That was the first time I had ever sat in a chauffeur-driven Rolls-Royce.

Having first exported our products to global markets, then tapped global financial markets for funds, the next logical step for us was to acquire a global manufacturing presence. I did that in 1998 with the purchase of Wallis Laboratory in Britain, and becoming a joint venture partner of Sidmark Laboratories in New Jersey, USA. Wallis was producing generic medicines. The acquisition of Wallis also gave me an opportunity to provide my son Murtaza with global experience. After completing his studies in the US, Murtaza had decided to partner with a friend and set up an IT company in the US. Though a student of medicine, IT was the rage at the time offering new business opportunities and he wanted to try his hand at it. Since he was not keen on returning home for a while, I suggested he get involved in Wallis in the UK and try his hand at running a part of the business abroad.

These were our early first steps in going global. But they gave us enormous confidence in our manufacturing capability, our organizational abilities and the worth of our R&D. A journey that had begun in the neighbourhood of Worli had now made its way to the world, and the next generation was beginning to learn the ropes.

There were several important lessons that I learnt from my early experience in managing our business. The idea that my father had instilled in me that one should not be afraid to make mistakes was constantly reinforced. I purged myself of fear by reminding myself that fear makes you die every day. I began to believe in myself even when I was up against the traditional advice of many elders. After all, it was they who had encouraged me in my youth to do what one believed in.

I was also struck by a famous Chinese saying that a path is created by walking. In other words, one must walk where others have not travelled, creating one's own path. When the business and policy environment one is used to changes, one must grab the new opportunities that a new environment offers rather than lament that the comfort of the familiar is no longer available. There is no advantage in resisting change. Of course, this attitude runs the inherent risk that with success there could also be failures. One must cherish the success and learn from the mistakes and the failures, and move on.

A visionary entrepreneur, business mentor and an industry leader and ex-president of the Rotary Club, Habil Khorakiwala wears numerous hats in his professional life of five decades. An alumnus of Purdue University and Harvard Business School, his mantra of 'Vision to Execution' has successfully led Wockhardt from infancy to being a major Indian pharmaceutical company and a global organization in the key economies of the US and the EU, with 'research and development' at its core. Wockhardt's pharmaceutical thrust has been in the areas of complex drugs, biotechnology and the development of next-generation antibiotics.

Habil Khorakiwala's efforts have significantly impacted availability of affordable medicines for the masses; and his successful acquisitions in India as well as globally, have catapulted Wockhardt into a leadership position in various international markets: in the UK, as the top-ranked Indian and among the top three generic companies; in Ireland, as the top-ranked generic company; and in the challenging US market, Wockhardt is placed at a highly-competitive position.

The Indian pharmaceutical industry has benefited immensely from Habil's leadership and out-of-the-box thinking. What symbolizes his major contribution as an industry leader is that as president of FICCI, he shared India's business and economic dynamics, with many presidents, prime ministers and heads of states, and his belief that India will emerge as a global leader in healthcare, not just in manufacturing but also as an R&D destination.

Habil pursues this dream even today; with faith in the competency and capabilities of Indian scientists, he is confident that India will soon launch advanced drugs and next-generation antibiotics; and he is passionately working to serve his country towards achieving this distinction.

Habil Khorakiwala has much more to his credit than the so-far-mentioned achievements and work-in-progress activities. His astute thought leadership and vision led to Wockhardt's diversification into one of the finest superspeciality hospital groups in the country with the belief: 'Life Wins'.

With his yearning for CSR, Habil has created the Wockhardt Foundation and evolved it into an organization structured and dedicated to today's primary social needs. In addition to his duties, he is also currently the chancellor of Jamia Hamdard University, New Delhi; Chairman of Governors at the Centre of Organization and Development, Hyderabad; a member of the World Economic Forum and a regular at Davos; and served as an Honorary Consulate of Sweden in Mumbai.

An active Rotarian, he being a member of the Arch C. Klumph Society represents his compassion, passion and commitment for Rotary, especially Bombay North. Amongst other benevolent activities, he has contributed $250,000 to the Rotary Foundation—the highest at the international level.

For one who lives such a fulfilling life, accolades are no rarities. His alma mater Purdue University bestowed on him the prestigious 'Distinguished Alumnus' title for significant contribution to the profession of pharmacy, and honoured him with an honorary doctorate. He is the only non-American and the first Indian in the 125-year history of the university to be awarded this honour.

**Vijay Lazarus**, former president, Rotary Club

# Chapter 4

## Multiple Missions

*If you want something new, you have to stop doing something old.*

—Peter Drucker

Over the last five decades I have lived a wonderful journey of learning, imbibing and creating different pathways. I have evolved continuously these past fifty years and so has Wockhardt. For the company, the past fifteen to twenty years in particular have been momentous. It has not been a smooth journey, but it has been a rewarding one. In any corporate adventure one encounters both opportunities and obstacles, success and failure. My urge to keep going has helped us climb mountains and walk untrodden paths. Early in life, I recognized that success has to be valued and preserved, yet I should not be afraid to experiment and to travel a path that is different.

From this idea emerged my first learning in the art of management—that one must always have one foot on surer ground while placing the other on the untrodden one. Balance risk and opportunity. For example, moving from Mumbai, a familiar geography and a single location, to new and many other locations in India and then abroad, required us to gradually change the way we managed our business and people. Managing a single-location business is very different from managing one that is spread across several geographies. If one foot is stable on a familiar geography, the other feels more confident in coming down on uncharted terrain.

*Dream come true: Habil Khorakiwala meeting Mother Teresa and receiving from her the Shiromani Vikas Award for Outstanding and Inspiring Contribution towards National Development*

The same principle holds for technology. One must secure mastery over the existing before experimenting with the new. We strengthened our organization by moving from one technology to another—from pharmaceutical formulations to bulk drug manufacturing, to large aseptic manufacturing, nutrition, biotechnology and so on. These changes can be accomplished with leaders and managers who have expertise and knowledge in the field. Therefore, culturally it is important to trust them, to empower them on the one hand and to develop organizational processes to monitor their performance and outcome on the other. From a management point of view what this means is that one must instil adequate confidence in one's senior colleagues and in what they are already doing so as to encourage them to do something new.

Growth requires acquisition of new knowledge (which comes embodied in people), new technology, new markets, new geographies, new businesses and new science. Often, one is moving forward on each of these fronts simultaneously. This approach enabled me in the first two decades to establish a credible base for creating an organization that has the competency to deal with various technologies. We built a sales and marketing organization for businesses all over the country and that enabled us to sustain decent and continuous growth and post adequate profitability.

Another important principle that defined my growth strategy was to deal with competition through increasing complexity. A complex organization and a multifaceted business structure can deal with competition more effectively than a simple organization catering to a single market. Of course, I never underestimated competition and all our strategies were built around the idea of handling existing and potential competition. Finally, one must always be willing to change and be open to change. These simple ideas defined every one of our missions. As we moved up the value chain and the ladder of complexity and entered new product lines and markets, we continued to adhere to these basic principles of management.

❧

I would not say that merely because I studied pharmacy in college I was destined to end up in the pharmaceutical business. After all, the Khorakiwala family was into many things and I grew up in a household that saw its main line of business as being retail. Sure, we had a drugstore, but that was retail business too. Many from my pharmacy college in Ahmedabad went on to do other things in life. I guess I was genuinely interested in the field, which was why I went on to secure a master's degree in pharmacy from Purdue. Setting up a pharmaceutical formulations manufacturing facility was, therefore, the logical thing to do. When I look back at the trajectory of Wockhardt, I realize that pharmaceutical has remained our core business even though we have from time to time branched out and also widened our ambit. Our next steps into nutrition, large volume injectables, biotechnology and drug discovery remained very much within the core. So too, in a way, the hospitals business. However, in arriving at this point, we have traversed many paths and built on our learning.

*Habil Khorakiwala felicitating Joseph Boyd Martin,*
*dean of Harvard Medical School, during the inauguration of*
*Wockhardt's first hospital in Mumbai*

I started with formulations and then moved into bulk drugs. That was a logical extension of the pharma business, but this second step required some additional learning on my part. After all, as a student of pharmacy I was au fait with formulations. But bulk drugs manufacture required a knowledge of chemical engineering and of relevant technologies that I was not very familiar with. This required hiring talent. Though the growth process was organic, from formulations to bulk drugs, it was contingent on the induction of skilled professionals in a field that I was new to.

After we found our feet in formulations and bulk drugs, a third wave of expansion came with our decision to enter the nutrition business. Interestingly, in those days we still regarded ourselves as being part of the 'pharma industry' and even the government viewed 'drugs and pharmaceuticals' as a single industry group. But when I began to consider the move into nutrition I realized that we were really in what is now widely referred to as the 'healthcare' business. Nutrition too was new technology and I had to learn a lot about the business, the markets and the technology.

In 1989 we made our next move, entering the business of manufacturing large volume parenterals (LVP). An LVP is a solution packaged in bags or bottles and administered through an injectable into the body in a variety of ways including intravenous. LVP is technically a part of the pharmaceuticals business but different because it is almost always administered by a doctor or nurse in a hospital setting. Hence, the market for LVP is the healthcare sector and LVPs are largely marketed directly to hospitals.

Even as we widened our business interests, we remained firmly embedded in manufacturing and in what I would call a 'doctor-oriented' business. Our expansion was based on the belief that growth comes not just with quantitative expansion of capacity in one line of activity but also, perhaps more importantly, through an expansion of the 'space' of our operations—market space and product space. The mastering of technology that such an expansion requires helps reduce costs and also opens up new possibilities through the learning-by-doing process.

But be it pharmaceutical formulations or the nutrition business or LVP, our customer was mainly the doctor. In bulk drugs we were either our own customers or there were other firms. Although the doctor was at the heart of the LVP business, our entry into this field came with an interesting learning that changed the way we had to conduct our business. The pioneer in the LVP business in India was Sushil Handa of Core Pharmaceuticals. Sushil was a highly talented and competent businessman. He maintained his dominant position in the market by ensuring that he ran a low-cost manufacturing organization. He exploited scale economies, went in for automation, invested in innovation and used his large capacity to keep manufacturing costs very low. He declared his objective to be market dominance and not just market leadership. His strategy acted as an entry barrier to any significant competition, ensuring and sustaining that market dominance.

There was only one chink in Handa's armour. His was a start-up company that required assured cash flow to service debt. So he created a marketing model that would ensure cash inflows. He appointed distributors who in turn appointed stockists who in turn dealt with retailers. This chain ensured that the manufacturer got his cash quickly even if the product remained in the marketing pipeline. However, it inflated the cost of selling. This weakness was exacerbated by the fact that he appointed a large number of sales persons to push the product and ensure its dominance in the market. That further raised the selling cost of his LVP output.

Having decided to enter the LVP market, I began studying the market and Core's strategy. I was impressed by Sushil's manufacturing strategy but identified a flaw in his marketing strategy. While the margin available for competition through cost was virtually non-existent, Core had such high marketing costs that there was scope for competition and a new entrant could fight for space. So I decided to change the game.

Since Core's strength lay in its low cost of manufacturing, I decided to try competing with it by reducing the overall cost of business. In other words, I found that I could enter the market by adopting a more efficient sales strategy. Instead of his two-layered marketing model—distributor and stockist—I used a single layer—only stockist—that we had in place across the country for our pharma business. He had a thousand sales representatives marketing his product. I hired no more than a hundred and fifty and focused only on big customers that together accounted for almost 70 per cent of the market. We brought the middlemen between the manufacturer and the doctor down to one, drastically reducing our marketing costs compared to the competition. I was able to enter the market by paying the stockist a little more than what he was able to because he also had a distributor to share his margins with. I was also able to use our product representatives, who would deal directly with doctors to sell LVP along with our pharma products. I gave them full freedom to negotiate a reasonable price directly with the consumer. His was a low-cost manufacturing strategy. Mine was a low-cost business strategy.

∽

Even as I was planning to divest out of LVP, I had heard that Fresenius AG of Germany was going to enter the Indian market. If they did, the valuation of Wockhardt's LVP business would drop. We would become number three in the Indian market. A multinational has deep pockets and the capacity to incur initial loss in an emerging market to acquire market dominance in the long run. If I was to divest then I should do so from my number two position, because that position would give us good valuation for our equity. I had been informed that Fresenius was planning to enter India by buying a Chennai-based firm, R.R. Medi Pharma. I had considered doing that myself a few months earlier and had realized that it would not be worth the price. I was confident I would retain my number two position even without acquiring R.R. Medi, though doing so would have given us a firmer foothold in southern India.

But if Fresenius entered India by buying R.R. Medi that would spoil my plans. It would give Fresenius a toehold from where they would expand. I had to think on my feet and act quickly. I called V. Raman of R.R. Medi and asked him if he was still willing to sell his facility to me and he immediately agreed. Clearly he was unaware of Fresenius's plans.

I asked him to quote a price. He quoted a figure that was double the price at which R.R. Medi was then listing on the markets. I immediately agreed. I had done my homework and knew that even at that price the deal would be worth it.

All this on the telephone, in just one straight conversation. I invited him to come down to Mumbai the next morning to sign the deal. He was surprised at my hurry but agreed to come. Over lunch, we drafted an initial term sheet and I requested him to sign it. He wanted to consult a friend of his in Chennai, Girinath, a member of his board. He wanted to return home before signing the final deal. I was not willing to wait. I suggested he at least initial the term sheet and that we could do the formal signing later. He finally agreed.

After returning home he called me to fix the auspicious date and time for the signing of the final agreement.

He ended that conversation saying, 'Habil, you did a smart thing!'

I wondered what he meant. Raman explained that when he had left Mumbai to return home he had met a representative of Fresenius at Chennai airport, on arrival. He had obviously been tipped off that Raman was in talks with me and wanted to make the offer that Fresenius had been planning to make. Raman had to tell him that he had already signed a deal with me!

I narrate the LVP story to make the point that in our business journey we were always very strategic in our thinking. I was not pursuing growth for the sake of growth. There had to be a purpose. My aim was to pursue organic growth, building on our core competence and deepening our capability and widening our reach. Having established the base in formulations and bulk drugs, our next step was to acquire global exposure and experience. Then we focused on strengthening our foundation in biotechnology and drug discovery. I have discussed these experiences in other chapters. Suffice it to say here that LVP was a transient opportunity that helped me learn more about the business and establish the infrastructure of domestic marketing.

⁂

I have no formal management education and hence I developed a habit of reading management literature and keeping abreast of developments in management practices and theories. I regularly attended executive development programmes in India and abroad and developed a personal rapport and link with some of the teachers from whom I learnt a lot and whom I respected. One of them was B.L. Maheshwari, who remained a teacher and guide to me for over a decade, and with whose help we introduced the concept of 'management by objectives' (MBO) in the late seventies and early eighties. This enabled us to grow simultaneously in many areas. We developed capacity over time to do more and more things differently. This was not a change for the sake of change. This was a change for growth, adopting new competencies in technology, in complexity of management, and in understanding different customer groups.

The principle is one of balancing risk, continuing to do what one is already doing but acquiring the competence to move forward in a new area, building on the strengths one has. For example, when we started the manufacture of and developed the technology for bulk drugs, we began with developing technology and setting up a manufacturing facility for dextropropoxyphene because we were ourselves using and importing this active substance at that time. Therefore, we were only acquiring the technology and not marketing the active pharmaceutical ingredient (API). That is how we acquired new technologies. Another example was bringing in new technology for infant nutrition. We already had the customers—paediatricians and gynaecologists.

Three important factors guided the strategically diverse businesses that we chose to enter into, build and grow. The first was to address the needs of the same customer group with different solutions. The second was the competitive advantage that would result in. And the third was an unintended but positive outcome, which was that by the early to mid-1990s, we had just over 20 per cent of our turnover being covered by the products coming under the government's restrictive Drug Price Control Order of 1987. This meant that an overwhelming 80 per cent of our turnover came from freely priced products.

Our nutrition business began with the plant in Halol, Gujarat, and then we added a plant near Chandigarh. Although we eventually divested this whole business to Danone, it was a space that we had entered with much thought and in which we had systematically built our presence. In the dietetic foods and infant formulae, one of Wockhardt's main products was Dexolac. We also had a strong presence in the infant antidiarrhoea market with the soya- and casein-based Nusobee line of products. At its peak, we held around 26 per cent of the market share for infant antidiarrhoea products based on soya and casein. We also got into a range of related infant products like rice-based weaning milk cereal that we marketed as Dexolac Milk Cereal and the other was Encal, a calcium supplement. We also came out with an offering called Lactofeed. It was a starter and a follow-up nutritional formula.

Our in-house R&D enabled us to develop our own process for new bulk drugs so that we were able to independently launch these drugs in the home market. By then, our R&D work had already gained national recognition. In 1988, the Indian Ministry of Science and Technology recognized these efforts by awarding our R&D division the First National Award for R&D Efforts. The appreciation of our research work by our national science and technology leadership greatly inspired us all. It also helped me build close friendships with a large number of eminent scientists including R.L. Mashelkar, who has remained a lifelong source of inspiration and support for Wockhardt R&D. It was, therefore, quite natural that in September 2004 we invited President A.P.J. Abdul Kalam to inaugurate our state-of-the-art Wockhardt Biotech Park in Aurangabad.

*Former President of India A.P.J. Abdul Kalam at the inauguration of the Wockhardt Biotech Park, the company's largest biotech research centre and manufacturing facility, in Aurangabad. Left to right: Habil Khorakiwala's daughter-in-law, Umaima; daughter Zahabiya; wife, Nafisa; Habil Khorakiwala; A.P.J. Abdul Kalam; daughter-in-law, Samina; son, Huzaifa; father, Fakhruddin T. Khorakiwala; son, Murtaza*

President Abdul Kalam's visit to the Wockhardt Biotech Park was a truly fulfilling experience for us all. He went around the facilities and took a keen interest in the research we were doing. He appreciated the fact that we had built what was perhaps the largest biopharmaceutical complex in India, with six dedicated manufacturing plants and R&D facilities. He appreciated the fact that not only had we been early movers in biotechnology and genomic research, but that we had built comprehensive capabilities in all facets of recombinant biotechnology. A.P.J. Abdul Kalam had particular interest in the field given his own contributions to the development of biotechnology. He was also very interested in the work we were doing in gene cloning and the construction of production strains, expression of proteins in all major systems (yeast, bacterial and mammalian cells) and their purification and pharmaceutical production.

⁌⁍

We began to build on our strengths in areas beyond our existing synthetic, chemistry-based pharmaceutical business. We explored, entered and expanded operations in a range of new areas. The link running across them was the fact that they all touched people. Our move into biotechnology was also a novelty at the time. Few pharma companies had moved into biotech manufacturing, though over the years biotech has become a natural fit for the pharma sector.

In biotech manufacturing, we developed and launched in India some of the vital recombinant biopharmaceuticals such as a hepatitis B vaccine (marketed as Biovac B), human erythropoietin (marketed as Wepox) and human insulin (marketed as Wosulin). What gives me particular satisfaction is the fact that Wockhardt was the first company in Asia to develop recombinant human insulin and is the fourth producer in the world, after Novo Nordisk, Eli Lilly and Boots. By 2003, we were able to manufacture and market our own recombinant human insulin. It was a defining and emotional moment for me.

Close on the heels of this work we also developed and mastered the technology to make a recombinant long-acting human insulin analogue, glargine. This made us the first company in the world after the innovator Sanofi Aventus to launch glargine (marketed as Glaritus). Today, it is available to patients in reusable and disposable pen delivery devices. Incidentally, Wockhardt is one of the few companies in the world to patent the technology of pen-based insulin delivery devices, which is the most preferred mode of insulin injections today. It is no wonder then that over the years Wockhardt has built a comprehensive diabetes management portfolio that includes insulin, oral medications, blood glucose monitors and diabetes nutrition products.

Currently, led by Maharaj Kishen Sahib, we have a team of around fifty people focused on R&D of biotech products, a pipeline of products that have been approved by the regulator in India and three to four products under development.

*Habil Khorakiwala receiving the Ernst & Young (EY) Entrepreneur of the Year Award from Infosys founder N.R. Narayana Murthy in 2004; also seen is Rajiv Memani, CEO and Regional Managing Partner of EY in India (extreme right)*

If my objective had only been to remain in the bulk drugs and formulations business, making use of the space provided by India's patenting regime, I would not have ventured into hospitals. However, I was clear in my mind that at some stage we had to graduate to become a research-based biotech and pharma company. This, along with our family's philosophy of pursuing socially relevant business, encouraged me to set up a medical centre in Kolkata in 1989. Our first foray into this space was as early as in 1973 when we set up First Hospitals and Heart Institute in Mumbai. At the time we were among the pioneers in corporate healthcare in India. But it was the 1991 decision to open the Wockhardt Hospitals and Heart Institute in Bengaluru that was our first serious move into healthcare. We entered the superspecialities space, specializing in cardiology, cardiac surgery and kidney transplants. The Kolkata operation expanded with the creation of the Wockhardt Hospital and Kidney Institute in 1993. Initially, we did not expand our presence in this space partly because we needed to understand it better given the complexity of a hospital business; it is not a product-making business and there are nuances involved with clinicians and protocols. We were in a sense perfecting ourselves in this sphere. Therefore, expansion was not the objective of the business at that point in time.

But I woke up to the opportunity we had created by happenstance. In April 2000, a team from Harvard Medical International—now known as Partners Harvard Medical International—a non-profit arm of Harvard Medical School, was visiting India. They were touring various regions looking at opportunities to offer advice on quality upgrades at healthcare facilities in developing countries. Their focus was on patient care and on value addition to services that would benefit patients. Among the many hospitals they picked for evaluation was our heart care hospital in Bengaluru. It was an eighty-bed facility doing mostly cardiac surgeries and angioplasties.

The team met me after their visit and said that they wished to collaborate with Wockhardt Hospitals. By then they had met all the large healthcare groups in India, including the big ones like Apollo. Given the relatively small size of our operation at the time I was taken aback by the level of their interest. My first question was, why us?

Their response was electrifying. The leader of the team, Robert Krone, was economical with his words. He came straight to the point. He said that he was impressed by our value system and our corporate philosophy. It matched their own thinking. Later, the dean of Harvard Medical School, Joseph Boyd Martin, visited us and inaugurated our hospital in Mulund, Mumbai. It was the first time ever that a dean of Harvard Medical School had visited India.

To be chosen by Harvard Medical School was a feather in our cap. We would be securing the imprimatur of Harvard. But what appealed to me more was the immense learning experience this would entail. Of course, the offer came with a price tag. We had to pay a fee of $250,000 for the service. We greatly benefited from the suggestions they offered to improve our standard operating procedures, hospital design, nursing training and all the other elements that go to make a world-class hospital. This exercise is annual and helps us constantly improve the quality of care.

I have always felt and said to my children and colleagues that I run my hospitals business with my heart and my pharma business with my head. Fortunately, I found a committed leader willing to take this vision forward. My daughter Zahabiya decided she would take charge of the hospital project. It was a moment of great joy and satisfaction for me. Like most fathers, I too have a soft corner for my daughter. She is not only my only daughter, but also the youngest. When my sons were growing up, I was far too busy and was unable to spend with them the kind of time I was later able to spend with Zahabiya.

Zahabiya finished her graduation from New York University and came back to Mumbai, where she invested three to four years (between 2004 and 2008) in setting up and running her own business. She had returned home with a desire to set up her own venture. She invested in a bubble tea business, selling a fruit-flavoured drink that had tapioca balls in it. Nafisa and I quite liked it. Zahabiya had been introduced to this drink in New York and felt Mumbai's globetrotting and trendy consumers offered a potential market. She set up a café in Bandra and it took off well. Marketing was a challenge and creating awareness about the product was not easy. She decided to divest and headed to Hyderabad to pursue an MBA programme at the Indian School of Business.

Even as she busied herself with her project and her studies she got married. Her husband, Ali Nabee, is a successful entrepreneur running a business out of Dubai and Mumbai. Zahabiya had to shuttle between Dubai and Mumbai. During one of her visits in 2010, I casually asked her if she would be willing to get involved with our hospitals business. To my great relief and utter happiness, she agreed.

Our hospitals business had by then expanded. The centre in Bengaluru was bigger and another important facility had come up in Mulund. We had built close to twenty hospital facilities, including in Tier 2 cities like Nagpur, Nashik and Rajkot. The business was now big and dispersed and needed attention at the top.

By 2008, we were operating the second largest private hospital chain after Apollo Hospitals. It was a position that we later ceded to Fortis when they bought up our facilities in Mumbai and Bengaluru. In fact, Fortis's best performing hospitals today are still our old Mulund and Bengaluru facilities. The divestment to Fortis was of course an emotional decision for me and for all of us at Wockhardt. It was a pragmatic business decision taken at a time when our focus was on the consolidation of our pharma and biotech business. In consolidating our businesses after the financial crisis of 2008, we sold ten of our seventeen hospitals. While we exited out of Mulund and Bengaluru, we retained our presence in Nagpur, Rajkot and Surat. As of 2017, we are building two new facilities in Mumbai—each a 350-bed facility.

When we launched our new facility in South Mumbai in 2015, I asked Zahabiya to choose a logo that would communicate our approach to the business. She worked with an advertising firm and came up with a winning pitch. I liked it. But it occurred to me that the phrase Zahabiya had chosen applied not just to our hospitals business but to everything else that Wockhardt did. I felt it ought to be our corporate logo. The two simple words capture the essence and the purpose of our multiple missions—Life Wins.

I have never pursued business growth for the sake of growth. Growing the business was the means to an end and not an end in itself. The ends I sought were new learnings—from research, from new drug discovery, new markets and new businesses. Each of these create new value. I believe growth and value creation are two sides of the same coin. Both are needed together. Growth without value creation is not sustainable.

As I ventured into each of our new missions and new projects, I was willing to take risks by embracing expansion and by seeking new learning. Of course, all this enables one to keep a step ahead of the competition. But new learnings do more than that. They create a knowledge-based organization that renews itself constantly. That is what growth enabled. I am proud that Wockhardt has grown to be a knowledge-based company that creates value and expands the boundaries of the possible.

I have known Habil Khorakiwala for over a decade now. He is one of the most warm-hearted and selfless business leaders I have ever met. While being a complete professional, he exudes personal warmth.

Wockhardt Hospital in Nagpur has played an important role in the treatment of poor people from my constituency, Chhindwara, and the culture in the hospital has been one of compassion while dealing with the poorest of the poor.

I once asked Habil how he could serve the people of my constituency and he introduced me to his son, Huzaifa Khorakiwala, who ran a mobile ambulance service for many years. Habil is one of the few distinctive personalities among our business leaders. He is not a run-of-the-mill entrepreneur and his personality stands out as one of a kind.

I wish Habil the best on the occasion of his 75th birthday.

**Kamal Nath**, Member of Parliament, former Union Minister of Commerce and Industry

Chapter 5

# Big on Basics

*Never innovate to compete, innovate to change the rules of the game.*

—David O. Adeife

*Wealth in the new regime flows directly from innovation, not optimization; i.e., wealth is not gained by perfecting the known, but imperfectly seizing the unknown.*

—Kevin Kelly

*W*hen you see all those drugs meant to control blood pressure, keep blood sugar in check, fight pain and provide relief from infections at a pharmacy, spare a thought for what it takes to bring a new medicine into the market. Drug discovery research is an arduous journey strewn with more risks than rewards. It is a multidisciplinary research effort spanning twelve to fifteen years, depending on the complexities associated with the new drug and its therapeutic area.

Typically, a discovery and development team comprises medicinal chemists, analytical chemists, drug scale-up experts, formulation development pharmacists, pharmacologists, microbiologists (for antiinfective drugs), toxicologists, veterinarians (to manage the uninterrupted supply of laboratory animals such as mice, rats, rabbits, guinea pigs, dogs, etc.) drug pharmacokinetics and metabolism experts. All of this to scientifically arrive at a therapeutic dose selection. These specialists are then aided by regulatory experts for regulatory submissions and by clinicians who design clinical studies. Finally, bio-statisticians are required to statistically validate the outcome of the safety and efficacy of a new drug. They do this by analysing clinical trial data involving thousands of patients. Thus, each stage in this journey, starting from the discovery of a promising compound to finally launching a new drug in the market, requires a lot of interdisciplinary interaction.

Over the years, the scientific complexity associated with drug discovery research has been growing due to various factors such as: (a) heightened expectations of new drug performance and safety by doctors and patients; (b) companies seeking differentiated products to withstand market competition; and (c) regulators seeking detailed profiling of drugs in terms of safety and efficacy, to safeguard society from any ill-effects of new drugs.

At Wockhardt, where we began our drug discovery programme in 1997, we have focused on the discovery of novel antibacterial drugs keeping in view the criticality of these factors in the discovery and development of global products. Today, we can claim to have an end-to-end antibacterial discovery and development capability, as well as a comprehensive antibacterial pipeline.

Wockhardt spends 12 to 13 per cent of its gross revenue on R&D. In recent years, we have not only increased R&D spending sharply but have sustained it despite problems on the financial front. In 2016, our total R&D investment was ₹6.7 billion, an increase of 30 per cent over the previous year. This also meant we had more than doubled our R&D investment in the three fiscal years 2013–16 as compared to the previous three fiscals: 2010–13. And all this only in our listed entity. There is a lot of work, as you will soon see, that is under way in our hospitals segment, especially in stem cells, the next frontier in healthcare.

## Chart 2: Schematic representation of the drug discovery process (pre-discovery stages)

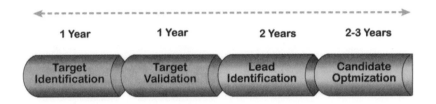

### Chart 3: Drug discovery and development

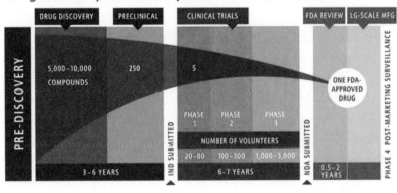

*IND: Investigational New Drug Application; NDA: New Drug Application; FDA: Food and Drug Administration (of USA)*

At a very broad level, there are three kinds of R&D activities that Wockhardt Limited is involved with today. One is the very generic Abbreviated New Drug Application (ANDA)-based research, which is mainly targeted at launching generic versions of innovator medicines in a market like the United States. An ANDA, an often-used term in the pharma world, is made by a company in the US for seeking an approval to launch in the market a generic version of an already existing licensed medicine or an innovator drug.

The second area of our R&D spending is biosimilars like insulin, glargine and others. The regulatory pathway for insulins in the US is now established.

The third area of R&D spending is the one that excites us all the most: new drug discovery. It is on the new chemical entity (NCE) front. But largely, it is breakthrough antibiotics that we are focused on. As we have seen, be it in India or even globally, this is an area that pharmaceutical companies have not given as much importance to as it deserves. Many have instead chosen to focus on lifestyle diseases. So far our R&D expenditure in the new drug discovery space has remained at around 10 per cent of our total R&D costs. But going forward, we will be spending millions of dollars in conducting the clinical trials for our breakthrough drug candidates. In the next couple of years, it could be as much as $150 million. We have filed more than eight hundred patents globally. Of these, 181 have been granted so far over the past fifteen years. Within these, the highest number of forty-seven patents have been granted in the US alone.

Crucial for any research activity is getting the right kind of people. We at Wockhardt have been fortunate in being able to build an excellent team of scientists and researchers. Innovation is as often an act of chance as it is of pursuit and perseverance. In managing a biotechnology, pharmaceuticals and healthcare business one is always in pursuit of talented and gifted professionals.

Serendipity also plays its role in enterprise. Sometimes one meets a professional who goes on to play a key role in one's business by sheer chance. One day in early 2012, my friend Udayan Patel, a psychoanalyst by profession, introduced me to the doctor who had successfully treated him for idiopathic pulmonary fibrosis. It is a condition in which there is progressive decline of the lung function because of the gradual thickening of lung tissues. I knew Udayan had been unwell for some time. It was, sadly, a very debilitating illness and I would feel very helpless looking at his condition. He had reached a stage where he could not even take ten steps without gasping for breath and had to wear an oxygen mask.

So I was surprised to find him in good spirits and health when I met him after a six-month gap. I had been told earlier that the doctors had given him barely three to six months to live. But, here he was in fine fettle. What was the secret of Udayan's improved health, I wondered. Udayan credited it to a scientist working in a small company. Vijay Sharma had an impressive track record behind him. For the past twenty years, he had been involved in stem cell research at various organizations.

Udayan decided to try his luck with Sharma. The procedure did not appear very complicated. Fat or adipose was extracted from Udayan's body and from it, stem cells were isolated. These were then put back into his body. The treatment worked. Udayan slowly regained his physical capabilities. He was able to walk for an hour and talk normally without getting breathless.

The joy of seeing Udayan recover gave way to intense curiosity. I wanted to meet the man who had made this possible. I also started educating myself on the latest thinking on stem cells. Many had already come to believe that stem cell-based treatment was the science of tomorrow. Like antibiotics in the 1940s, stem cell-based treatment was the next wave in medical treatment. It became clear to me that Wockhardt had to invest in this field and that I had to hire Vijay Sharma. I invited him to join us as director of stem cell research at Wockhardt Hospitals.

There are good reasons why I strongly feel that stem cell-based treatment is the future. Without stem cells, wounds would never heal, your skin and blood would not continually renew themselves, fertilized eggs would not grow into babies, and babies would not grow into adults. Stem cells are quite unlike the specialized, or differentiated, cells in your body—such as the nerve cells, muscle cells and blood cells that enable you to function. In contrast, they are the body's silent reserves. At any given moment, many of the stem cells in your body won't be doing very much. They only spring into action when you need to either produce more stem cells or make more of other specialized types of cells. And they're not just found in humans.

Stem cells have the remarkable potential to develop into many different cell types in the body during early life and growth. In addition, in many tissues they serve as a sort of internal repair system, dividing essentially without limit to replenish other cells as long as the person or animal is alive. When a stem cell divides, each new cell has the potential either to remain a stem cell or become another type of cell with a more specialized function, such as a muscle cell, a red blood cell, or a brain cell.

Stem cells are distinguished from other cell types by two important characteristics. First, they are unspecialized cells capable of renewing themselves through cell division, sometimes after long periods of inactivity. Second, under certain physiologic or experimental conditions, they can be induced to become tissue- or organ-specific cells with special functions.

Stem cells are important for living organisms for many reasons. In the three- to five-day-old embryo, called a blastocyst, the inner cells give rise to the entire body of the organism, including all of the many specialized cell types and organs such as the heart, lung, skin, sperm, eggs and other tissues. In some adult tissues, such as bone marrow, muscle and brain, discrete populations of adult stem cells generate replacements for cells that are lost through normal wear and tear, injury or disease. In other organs such as the pancreas and the heart, stem cells only divide under special conditions. Given their unique regenerative abilities, stem cells offer new potentials for treating diseases such as diabetes and heart disease.

When I met Vijay, he gave me a wish list of the kind of resources and infrastructure he would need to lead stem cell research and application at Wockhardt. We did not stint in providing what was needed and I made sure we imported the best available equipment and that it was in place before he joined us. He was delighted to see that we had everything ready for him the day he joined us in June 2012. For me it was also a statement of trust. I had told him that while he loved science, I respected scientists. I had assured him that he would have my undivided attention whenever he needed it. I had to establish my credentials with him on day one.

Thanks to my association with several scientists and doctors I had learnt one important lesson. There is a fundamental difference between hiring and dealing with managers as opposed to researchers. In this field, we have professionals for whom goals are guided more on a quarter-to-quarter and year-to-year basis, like, say, those in finance and marketing. But then, along with them, there are others—researchers and scientists—for whom the time horizon can be a decade or two. Both function in a world of uncertainty. But the degree of uncertainty a finance manager has to deal with is far less than what a microbiologist has to deal with in developing a new drug. Managers tend to worry about work specifications, salaries, perks, reporting relationships and so on. These matter for a researcher as well, but his bigger concerns are around availability of equipment, infrastructure and the software needed for his research. A researcher seeks an organizational ecosystem that values his work, understands the challenges he faces and encourages him to do better research.

Managing both sets of talented people is a complex task. I reached out to my friend and management guru the late B.L. Maheshwari, to help me understand the process of doing this. At the time, Maheshwari was based at Hyderabad's Administrative Staff College of India. He later created his own institution, the Centre for Organization Development, with which I have been associated from the beginning. He helped me develop systems for performance assessment, with measurable goals in areas where quantitative numbers to measure performance are not available, like, say, in human resources (HR) or research, including writing out measurable objectives.

∽

Even when Wockhardt went through financial ups and downs, and we had our share of problems, I made sure that our support to R&D and to basic research was never found wanting. When I look back I have the satisfaction of knowing that not only was our money well spent but that our investment in research has paid off and will continue to do so.

I believe India has the potential to be the 'fifth hub' of research and development in pharmaceuticals and biotechnology, after the US, Europe, Japan and China. Big pharma has already established a hub in China; and in a way, that is what is different about the industry in China, as compared to in India, where the bulk of the business is still led by Indian companies. In fact, the Indian model of the dominance of domestic ownership over pharma companies is a fairly unique model. In most other countries, developed and developing, global multinationals dominate the pharma sector in terms of both ownership and market shares. Even in Japan, which has a sizeable and impressive domestic enterprise in pharma, global companies have a dominant position.

India has both the talent and the capabilities. What we have lacked for a long time is a supportive regulatory and fiscal environment. We have made it increasingly difficult for R&D groups to conduct clinical trials within India. A modern economy needs a science-based approach to research. In India, we still have an administrative and political approach to scientific research in the realm of medicine and biotechnology.

In countries like the US and UK, the procedure for conducting clinical trials is simple yet rigorous. One makes an application to the relevant regulatory institution and after due process the programme is cleared. In fact, one can meet the regulator before making an application so that there are no difficulties in processing. The authorities tell you what is acceptable to them, what modifications they want and they provide you with the recorded minutes of all the relevant discussions that took place during the application review process. One then knows what to do and what not to do. The whole process is based on good monitoring and trust. It is completely transparent and scientifically oriented.

Unfortunately, in India, we have complicated the process and made it very non-transparent. You apply for permission, the authorities take their own time to grant it, and even after it is granted, sudden changes are suggested. One day you are in the right, the next day you could be in the wrong. And so it goes on in circles. That is why at Wockhardt we decided that we would conduct our trials abroad.

In India we have also not sufficiently incentivized investment in R&D. The fiscal incentives that have been provided were neutralized by the minimum alternate tax (MAT). In Britain, for example, if a firm's investment in R&D results in the development of patents, and if such patented discoveries are converted into manufactured products that are then available to the consumer, the firm gets a tax break. I believe the tax rate falls sharply from 25 per cent or 30 per cent to as low as 10 per cent. That is an attractive incentive. It is the kind of fiscal incentive that promotes research, innovation and manufacturing.

Despite all the challenges I faced in investing in R&D I decided that Wockhardt had to be a research-based pharmaceutical and biotechnology company. Over the period 2006–16, we have invested on an average at least 10 per cent each year on R&D in Wockhardt Limited. This does not include the R&D spend of Wockhardt Hospitals. Finding professionals like Mahesh Patel, Maharaj Kishen Sahib, Vijay Sharma, Sachin Bhagwat, V.J. Patil, Ravikumar and others—each a scientist-cum-researcher-cum-patriotic Indian-cum-dedicated professional, all rolled into one—was my good fortune and the cornerstone of our enterprise. They have inspired younger colleagues and large teams that have remained committed to their professional work and loyal to the company. More importantly, one has to retain talent so that the best and brightest find enough space and time to do research and deliver results.

∽

For me, R&D is really about the ability to take risks and think long term. I have always felt that mindsets driven by notions of profit versus returns or risk-adjusted returns are not appropriate to undertaking this journey into the unknown. In most businesses we are able to acquire a fair approximation of risk and reward. Investments are made on the basis of projections about demand. In biotechnology and with healthcare products, uncertainty looms larger.

A research-based business organization should have three key attributes: first, clarity of purpose and long-term and steadfast commitment to that purpose; second, different ways to evaluate the performance of business managers and researchers; and third, dedicated commitment of top management to long-term research goals.

Over the years, I have had to balance considerations relating to good financial governance, returns to investors and the long-term interests of a company that seeks to build on the foundations of its research capability. Carrying together the expectations of my financial team, the financial institutions and members of my board while assuring our researchers that we remain invested in them even if results take time has been a challenge. Though I must admit that each of them, including members of my family, have remained fully invested in our dream to build a research-based firm. It is the trust of each one of the stakeholders and shareholders that has brought us to this threshold of a new dawn.

My first meeting with Habil took place in late 2002. He had moved to a temporary office after the collapse of Poonam Chambers in the summer of 2002, where his offices originally were. I had joined Harvard Medical International a few years ago and was in search of the right group, whose vision aligned with ours—a bold vision to work together to build a system that could help transform healthcare in India, which involved thinking beyond the issues of Return on Investment (ROI) and profits. Remember, this was not the India of today. We had good doctors but poor health systems. What was to be a fifteen-minute meeting lasted for about two hours. Habil discussed a vision of improving healthcare in ways I had not heard anyone before speak of in India. I left that meeting excited and sure that I had found the right partner in Habil.

This was the beginning of a long and rich friendship, and the relationship between us and our two entities that has lasted over fifteen years. Along the way, we have developed many unique programmes together, many of which have truly transformed healthcare in India: the first hospital to get international quality accreditation from the Joint Commission in the US, the first programme to educate frontline HIV health workers, the first national awards programme recognizing physicians who had left a lasting legacy in Indian healthcare, the first nurse leadership programme, and the list continues to grow... It has been an amazing journey together. In many ways, Habil's Wockhardt hospitals have become an exemplar for us in what can be done in healthcare, how it can be done, and what it needs to get it done.

I have grown to deeply admire Habil for so many of his amazing attributes and qualities. However, the things that absolutely stand out are: his vision and ability to see possibilities that others can't; his boldness and courage to act on his vision and convictions, where others shy off; his incisive mind that cuts through all the extraneous and superfluous issues to get to the heart of any matter; his commitment and the deep sense of friendship, generosity and trust, all of which that have allowed the relationship between our institutions to thrive over all these years and caused our friendship to deepen. Yet a leader's true mark of greatness is his ability to nurture and mentor the leaders of tomorrow. Over the years, Habil's team members have gone off and become leaders in healthcare in India. A number of them were responsible for helping craft the national standards for hospital quality accreditation; others are running major hospitals, yet others are part of global funds leading healthcare investments in India.

I often look back and am amazed at the ways in which Habil has actualized that original vision we talked about in his temporary office, decades ago. On this wonderful occasion of his 75th birthday, I wish him all the very best. We need more Habils in India!

**Mehul C. Mehta**, MD
Vice-President, Partners HealthCare International

Chapter 6

# Going Global

*Indian corporates are emerging as global players... I want Indian companies to go global.*

—Atal Bihari Vajpayee

*I*t was at the Pravasi Bharatiya Divas in January 2003 that Prime Minister Atal Bihari Vajpayee announced that Indian companies would henceforth be free to make overseas investments up to 100 per cent of their net worth, be it through overseas joint ventures or wholly owned subsidiaries. The existing restrictions on overseas investments by Indian companies were gone. Within months, in July 2003, we acquired CP Pharmaceuticals, a UK-based company. But, of course, by then we had already made our first foray into Britain. Wockhardt became the first Indian pharmaceutical company to buy a British pharma company when we acquired Wallis Laboratories in 1998.

The idea that we should go global was embedded in me almost two decades before I was ready to venture out. It was in the classrooms at Harvard University in the early 1980s, where I was enrolled for the Advanced Management Programme, that I was imbued with the belief that an Indian company ought to one day become a global multinational. At the time, that was not yet the general mood in the Indian pharmaceutical industry. Most of us were still seeking protection from external competition and were far too defensive to even contemplate going global.

*Habil Khorakiwala greeting former Prime Minister Atal Bihari Vajpayee*

The sentiment in India was best captured by what Prime Minister Indira Gandhi told the World Health Assembly in 1982, in Geneva. 'The idea of a better-ordered world is one in which medical discoveries will be free of patents and there will be no profiteering from life and death.' That official view was endorsed by the Indian Drug Manufacturers Association (IDMA) and many in the industry, led by Bhai Mohan Singh of Ranbaxy, supported a non-governmental organization called the National Working Group on Patent Laws (NWG), which lobbied in favour of India joining other developing countries like Brazil in opposing a US move to bring intellectual property rights and patents

under the purview of the General Agreement on Tariffs and Trade
(GATT).

*With 'can-mates' and lifelong friends from Harvard Business School. Sitting
(from left): L.E. Buzarde, John Harrish, Habil Khorakiwala, George Petty. Standing
(from left): John Vaughey, David Lovett, Renaud Terrence.*

I was not very active with this movement but kept myself informed
on policy debates. By the end of the 1980s a new body of opinion
began to be expressed from within Indian industry. Along with me,
Anji Reddy and Parvinder Singh began to voice a different point of
view. We rejected the very defensive and protectionist world-view
of the IDMA and NWG and argued that intellectual property rights
protection was in the interests of research-based drug development
in India, that Indian companies had the potential to get into drug
discovery and that the threat from MNCs should not be exaggerated.
The period between 1988 and 1991 saw intense debates on the issue
of the regulatory regime for global trade in pharmaceuticals and new
drug discovery.

Then, all of a sudden, the policy environment in India underwent a big change. In the summer of 1991, Prime Minister Narasimha Rao introduced radical new economic policies, liberalizing industrial and trade policies. He then proceeded to sign on to the creation of the World Trade Organization (WTO), with the attendant clauses on trade-related intellectual property rights protection. The writing was on the wall for us. To face global competition we must go global ourselves.

I also observed what was happening in the IT sector. That too was a knowledge-based industry, like pharmaceuticals. If Indian IT could compete globally, why not Indian pharma? Of course, the entry costs were far higher in pharma, but we in India had the advantage of low-cost high skills. Our scientists and biotechnologists were very talented. We call it the 'India Advantage'—world-quality human resources at India-levels of cost. Pharma was well placed to benefit from this.

But to become global, one must first go global. In other words, I had to first acquire global experience of running an established pharma company abroad before taking my own company abroad. I needed both the managerial experience of running a foreign company and an understanding of external markets. I knew that trade liberalization and scale economies would sooner rather than later force us to look for global markets. So I viewed the acquisition of firms abroad as a way of learning how business and markets work there. My interest was not just in serving a pre-existing Western market through a pre-existing but now acquired Western company, but to learn how to create a foreign market for an Indian company exporting to it. After all, we were investing in research at home and would come out with products that could secure a global market, provided we had adequate knowledge of such markets. If we wished to continue to invest in R&D we needed not just the funds for it but also a better understanding of the global market and the rules of the game by which global companies acquired global markets.

I knew that the US was the single biggest market for pharmaceuticals and my interest was initially in getting into the US market. But it was also the most difficult market to enter, in the case of pharma. So acquiring firms in the UK was the necessary first step to acquiring a firm in the US. It gave us an understanding of Western markets, and it also helped us create an external profile and personality for the Wockhardt brand. I was also advised by many, including McKinsey, to first acquire a European presence because the European market was a more attractive one with much higher drug prices than in the US. In those days we did not have direct flights to the US from India. On a journey from India to the US one had to touch down in Europe. That is what I did.

The successful acquisition of Merind Limited in 1998, a Tata group company in India, gave me both the experience and confidence to pursue the acquisition of the UK-based Wallis Laboratories the same year. Wallis had the advantage of being a private label manufacturer for pharmacy and over-the-counter retailers. It was valued at $9 million. The acquisition of Merind made Wockhardt the fifth largest pharmaceutical company in India. The acquisition of Wallis, the first such acquisition of a British firm by an Indian one, made 1998 a truly historic year for us. In calendar year 1999, our exports crossed the ₹1 billion ($22 million at the time) mark and Wockhardt posted an annualized sales growth of 43 per cent.

I devoted considerable time to understanding Wallis and the UK market and getting the staff at Wallis to understand Wockhardt. It was another five years before I made my next move. In 2003, we acquired CP Pharmaceuticals, by then a fifty-year-old British company producing generics and hospital drugs. CP Pharmaceuticals was a fully integrated pharmaceutical firm with four key business areas—hospital brands, generics, contract manufacturing and exports. It held 225 product licences and had a special manufacturing licence to manufacture patent-protected drugs under development. It also had the UK Home Office licence for the manufacture of schedule 1 controlled drugs.

To top it all, it had a USFDA approved injectable facility for the manufacture of injectables (vials, cartridges and ampoules).

Apart from the UK, the rest of Europe was also an important place to create business, as had been pointed out to me by several McKinsey consultants. At the time, the price of generics was significantly higher in Germany, France and other EU countries and competition was also relatively less. So we kept our eyes on Europe and acquired companies in Germany, Ireland and a significantly large acquisition in France. The French company was not a generic company but a branded one and I felt that for the future, the new learning should be on 'how to do branded business in a developed market'. Two things went wrong with this acquisition in France. First, the company did not provide complete disclosure; and second, we failed to perceive that the branded business would soon face competition from generics. This even after examining the patent position.

To deal with the disclosure issue we went for arbitration and won on that issue, but the compensation we secured was not very large compared to the purchase price we had paid. We also did not succeed in learning much about branded marketing and so I felt we did not achieve our original objectives.

Nonetheless, we made significant progress in our quest to go global; in the decade 1998–2007, we at Wockhardt signed on to six acquisitions in the global markets—two in the UK, three in Europe and one in the US.

✂

In going global my key learning has been that a company must have one way of doing things wherever it is located. One cannot allow multiple styles of management and work. When we bought CP Pharmaceuticals in 2003, I invited Sirjiwan Singh to take charge of the acquisition and operation. Sirjiwan had moved into contract manufacturing from

Merind. He had manufacturing experience. My need at the time was not on the financial side. We knew how to handle that. We needed someone who was familiar with manufacturing and could take charge of a going concern. We did try to engage local English managers but that did not work. I then picked someone from India—Sirjiwan—because I wanted someone who understood our culture and would be able to operate independently in a foreign land while remaining firmly embedded in our culture and way of doing things.

When we acquired CP Pharmaceuticals, I invited their entire senior staff for dinner and explained to them what the Wockhardt culture was. You have been part of a successful company, I said to them, but we have also been a successful company. Now we are all one company. You will have to get used to our style of functioning. If you are comfortable with that, you can stay. If you are not comfortable, you can go. To my pleasant surprise, we had very few exits after acquisition. On an average, perhaps 10 per cent of the existing staff chose to leave because they were not comfortable with the new style of working. But 90 per cent stayed on. They learnt to adapt to and adopt our culture and values. For me, that has always been the bottom line.

The success of this approach in the acquisition of CP Pharmaceuticals encouraged me to follow the same approach when we acquired Morton Grove in the US and Pinewood in Ireland. I have always believed that a successful company should not waste time integrating the cultures of the parent company and the newly acquired one. There is a great deal of management literature about integration after acquisition. We do not integrate. We assimilate.

When we moved into Europe and began acquiring firms there, I realized I needed someone with local language proficiency and an understanding of local work culture. Different geographies demand different solutions. That was an important lesson I learnt. As one globalizes and does business in different countries one must adapt to that environment without deviating too much from one's own preferred and established business culture and practices.

The United States was very different. The first thing that struck me was that both native Americans and non-resident Indians living in the US adopted a superior attitude when dealing with an Indian businessman. They believed that they were better educated, better trained, better equipped to manage a company, even if the owner was an Indian. I was convinced from my experience in the UK and Europe that there was no such iron law of global competence. I decided to send a senior colleague from India to head the US operations. Sunil Khera was head of our domestic business in India. I asked him to take charge of our North American business as president.

I was not even sure if Sunil had ever travelled to the US. However, in India he had an excellent track record of performance and great leadership. His additional qualification was that he knew Wockhardt well, and I knew him well. Sunil took our business in the US from less than $100 million to over $500 million in three years. He built the entire operation and the organization in the US.

In each of the countries where we have acquired buinesses, almost the entire staff—scientific, manufacturing, HR, marketing and finance staff—is local. We never took hundreds of Indians abroad. We hired everyone locally. But the leadership is Indian. That too, Indians who have trained in India and have worked in India with Wockhardt. They are our leaders—at home and abroad. Leadership matters. If you have the right person in the right place, you get results.

The purpose of an acquisition is to create value for the company. My focus has always been on what creates value, not on trying to integrate cultures. Wockhardt is what it is—be it in India, the UK, Germany, France or the US. There is a Wockhardt way of functioning, a Wockhardt way of creating value and everyone should feel that they are part of the same team engaged in a common endeavour.

∽

Today, apart from the US, Europe and India, Wockhardt has operations either directly or through partners or distributors in Russia, Mexico, Brazil, Vietnam, Myanmar, Thailand, the Philippines, Nepal, Egypt, Iran, Iraq, Lebanon and Sri Lanka apart from African countries such as Kenya, Ghana, Nigeria and Tanzania. Thus, our research effort is now truly global. For instance, we have fifteen to eighteen partners around the world including experts and contract research organizations. It is a multi-geographical and globally collaborative exercise, be it in relation to testing, safety or toxicology studies. It is integral to the whole antiinfectives drug discovery. For example, in the case of WCK 5222, it requires testing on a collection of strains worldwide and that too, recent strains.

The purpose of going global was not merely to access new markets and acquire good companies but also to access new knowledge and acquire greater competence. Towards this end we have encouraged our researchers to interact with their peers abroad and have their work evaluated critically and professionally.

An important institutional platform that Wockhardt's scientists have zealously participated in is that of Key Opinion Leaders (KOLs) in their fields of research. I attended our first KOL meeting in Chicago in March 2012.

The experience made me realize the value of these meetings and since then, I have tried to attend as many KOLs as possible. Our research centres in Europe offer us an excellent base for these meetings. KOL meetings serve an important purpose in this global journey of ours. They offer a professional forum at which experts and peer reviewers assess the work of our scientists, offer their comments and give our scientists an understanding of where they stand on the knowledge curve. This continuous and iterative process of interaction between our scientists and independent evaluators is key to the progress of our research effort. These internationally reputed experts have evaluated our work on antibacterial drug samples and have given us the confidence that we are on the right track.

There is another important purpose that KOL meetings and interactions serve. They help our scientists test their ideas with experts so as to be able to publish their research findings in professional journals. This is important for a scientist because even as we, as a company, engage in the process of drug discovery and development of products, they, our scientists, have to keep abreast of knowledge in the field of their research and constantly seek peer approval for their work. Such publications also serve the purpose of letting the world know that we are a credible research-based company. More to the point, the better-informed clinicians and doctors who keep track of research feel reassured when they see that a drug we are marketing is based on high quality research that has met the approval of peer-reviewed professional journals. This kind of independent scrutiny by independent global field experts is crucial for any new drug.

At each stage of medicine-making, be it a simple one or a complex process, we have to draw on the latest available knowledge, check our competence against global standards and then take the next step. Starting with the making of APIs or bulk drugs, then to formulations or consumable medicines, and moving on to ANDAs at every stage, we have to keep validating our steps against global best practices. The ultimate frontier in medicine is new drug discovery, based on research into new chemical entities (NCEs).

Wockhardt has filed the Investigational New Drug Applications (INDAs) for five NCEs in the US. Every single molecule has gone through Phase I study in the US. We aim to complete our Phase II study for WCK 4873 in 2017 and then decide the date for Phase III clinical trial. We plan to move for clinical trials, including in the US and Europe, for our WCK 5222 and WCK 4282, which is likely to be completed and approved by end 2020 or early 2021, hopefully. We at Wockhardt decided not to shy away from or be scared of big pharma. We took the lead, invested in drug development in the heart of the developed West, subjecting ourselves to all their regulatory supervision and discipline, and have come to the threshold of the final Phase III stage. When we cross that threshold, we would have arrived on the world stage based on our own intellectual capital.

If we had been just any other pharmaceutical company exporting medicines already patented or exporting generics and bulk drugs, then the process of going global would have been essentially a managerial journey. It would have involved finding markets, investing in subsidiaries and so on. Everyone does that. Anyone can do that. But, as we entered the new century, I took the decision that Wockhardt should be a research-based pharmaceutical company that invests in drug discovery and is able to market its products globally. Going global meant not just doing business around the world but also being linked with the global knowledge creation network.

This came across to me vividly at the American Society of Microbiology (ASM) event, Microbe 2016, in Boston, USA. Wockhardt made fifty-nine presentations. Display charts showed the work we were doing and seven oral presentations were made to a packed audience in large conference halls. That was the highest level of presentation in that year's conference made by a single firm. An informed and interested audience of over 15,000 listened to our scientists. As I sat there watching my colleagues speaking, I was filled with great emotion, a sense of joy and fulfilment, and recalled the words of Alan Kay: 'The best way to predict the future, is to invent it.' In our field of business, that is what we were doing.

Working for and with Habil Khorakiwala is a unique experience; it challenges you to know not only every technical and business detail, but also a practical way forward to implementing a solution. His optimism and creative force are always evident, and it is the principle source of inspiration and motivation for many who work for and with him.

His ability to inspire and motivate, I believe, is one of the secrets of his success—in taking Wockhardt Limited in the early 1960s from a small twenty-employee company to the global company it is today. The other secret of his success is his commitment to pharmaceutical research, which has always been steadfast and far-sighted. Today, this commitment is visible in the new antimicrobial drugs discovered by Wockhardt and progressed to clinical stage development to receive the USFDA's Qualified Infectious Disease Product status. His zeal for innovation and improvement, I believe, will continue to drive Wockhardt enterprises to offer the world several other innovative solutions for critical unmet medical and general human needs.

When I visit the Purdue University, I see his name prominently displayed as a Distinguished Alumnus, and I am not surprised to keep learning of his many awards, such as Outstanding and Inspiring Contributions toward National Development, which was presented to him by Mother Teresa. When you are working with him, you do not realize how much he has accomplished and the numerous awards he has received. I am often amazed by his simplicity.

I have been privileged to know him as a distinguished pharmaceutical entrepreneur, who continues to pave the way for affordable and innovative medicines from India to the world. I wish him all success and look forward to many new contributions by Wockhardt, inspired and materialized by his creative force, optimism and steadfast commitment to science and research. To those who work for and with him, I wish to remind them: you have an amazing opportunity to learn, so do your homework well and learn the why, how and what of success, not only in the context of self-interest but in the interest of humanity. To conclude this message,

I quote Mother Teresa: 'Be faithful in small things because it is in them that your strength lies.'

**Ajaz S. Hussain**, President-Founder,
Insight, Advice & Solutions, LLC, USA

## Chapter 7

# Risk and Reward

*An organization's capacity to improve existing skills and learn new ones is the most defensible competitive advantage of all.*

—C.K. Prahalad

usiness enterprise entails a constant attempt to balance risk and reward. The risks I had taken in the two decades leading up to the turn of the century were, on balance, rewarded more than I had ever imagined. The 1990s was a decade of growth and optimism for us at Wockhardt. It was a decade of joy in my family as we welcomed new members into our fold. We naturally entered the twenty-first century with a great deal of optimism. That mood was further enhanced by our outward expansion. The forays into new products, new technologies, new markets and new geographies gave us the confidence to take new risks. The experiments we were doing in our laboratories, the products we had launched and the acquisitions we had made abroad contributed to both organic and inorganic growth.

Success breeds ambition. Growth requires sustenance. We were fired by our ambitions but growth required financing. In search of funds we entered unconventional terrain. Globally, financial markets were introducing new products and new methodologies to raise funds and finance corporate expansion. Sure, the world economy as well as India's was going through ups and downs, but the mood of optimism in the first few years of the new century was infectious. Alan Greenspan, chairman of the US Federal Reserve Board, viewed in his time as a global financial czar, had dubbed the 1990s' stock market enthusiasm as 'irrational exuberance', but had done little to stem it. Much of that optimism continued into the early 2000s, especially after the United States bounced back from the 9/11 terror attack in New York.

This was also the period when we were acquiring businesses globally and needed finance to fund our acquisitions and market expansion. The head of finance at the time, an enthusiastic young man, Rajiv Gandhi, introduced me to the new world of derivatives and financial engineering. We entered into forward exchange contracts using derivative instruments purely as a hedging device to establish the amount of reporting currency required or available at the settlement date of certain payables and receivables. It was not our intention to trade or enter into speculative activities. In December 2006, we had entered into two contracts on outstanding currency swaps, in addition to forward exchange contracts, to hedge against fluctuations in changes in the exchange rate and interest rate.

I had traditionally been a conservative when it came to finance. I was willing to take risks with new products and in new markets, but never with raising and managing funds. However, I must confess I took my eye off the ball when it came to the issue of investing and trading in derivatives and delegated responsibility to Gandhi. It was in any case his responsibility to manage our foreign exchange transactions, given our growing global business and foreign currency loans. He assured me that he would do this without too much risk to the company, and would ensure that we incurred no foreign exchange loss; in fact, we may even generate some surplus.

The market environment was also infectious. Everyone was into derivatives and India risk was generally regarded as being low.

Remember that between 2003 and 2008, the Indian economy had unprecedented rates of high growth, recording an annual average rate of growth of close to 9 per cent. That was the half-decade of historically high growth for India and many foreign banks operating in India, including Citibank, were encouraging finance managers to invest in derivatives; they spoke to our people too. Gandhi was quite confident that he understood the issues and would be able to manage them. Since we were not the only company entering this new terrain, I assumed we were on safe ground.

The problem arose partly because of hasty decisions taken by the finance team at that time by getting into speculative trading, and partly, as I have been given to understand, because the foreign banks were actively overselling their products. The events of 2008 overtook us. It all began with the implosion at Lehmann Brothers in September 2008. Overleveraged US companies pushed several financial institutions, mainly in the US and the UK, into the red. Valuations collapsed, banks merged or shut down, major US multinationals were on the verge of bankruptcy. We too were hit by the financial crisis.

It was only when we were directly hit by the market collapse that I realized what Gandhi had been up to. I quickly reached out for expert advice. I first approached Hari Mundra, who had earlier worked with us as group financial director. I then consulted A.V. Rajwade, the well-known risk management specialist who had also written a book on derivatives. He was on various committees of the Reserve Bank of India and was very knowledgeable. Mundra and Rajwade brought me up to speed on the issues at hand and also showed me how we had been misled by the bankers advising us. These banks had not fulfilled their fiduciary responsibilities. I then hired Ponty Singh, who had been with Morgan Stanley and was then based in Singapore. He had a firm called Tricolor Capital Markets, and was known to be an expert in restructuring derivatives. He had a computer model to analyse the data, go into the history of the derivatives, the price at which derivatives had been sold at each iteration, check whether the risk was appropriate to the price charged and so on.

I studied the issue systematically with the help of these experts. I found myself in a catch-22 situation. I understood the problem, but the person who had to deal with the problem was the one who had in fact got us into it, in the first place. Should I ask the same person to now help us get out of the situation? I was not comfortable with that. This required me to keep a close eye on financial matters.

∽

These problems came on top of earlier financial issues that our growth ambitions had created. In the early 2000s, since the cash flow from existing business was not adequate to fuel our growth plans, and given our stellar credit rating, we decided to borrow. Our debt increased severalfold and stood at ₹42,351 million by 2008. So did the interest cost. We tried raising funds through an IPO for Wockhardt Hospitals, but the response was disappointing, forcing us to withdraw the offering.

At the time when the Reserve Bank of India had issued foreign currency convertible bonds (FCCBs), our shares were trading at prices far higher than the ones prevailing when they came in for redemption. Faced with the possibility of default I decided that we had to knock on a window that the Reserve Bank of India had opened a few years earlier for Corporate Debt Restructuring (CDR). What was disconcerting was the fact that few Indian companies had successfully come out of a CDR process till date.

I realized we had made mistakes. But then, I recalled my father's advice. Do not worry about making a mistake. But never repeat it. I decided that we had to take a step back and make amends. I recalled the way India had handled the financial crisis of 1991. Prime Ministers Chandra Shekhar and P.V. Narasimha Rao had wasted no time in mortgaging gold to avert default. Nothing focuses the mind like a crisis does. The important thing was not to default. I decided we too had to sacrifice some of our family silver—or more like our crown jewels—so to speak, to restore financial health as quickly as possible. It was a bitter pill to swallow. I knew that there was nothing fundamentally wrong with Wockhardt. Not only was our core business sound but its inorganic growth trajectory stood out as the path to take. The reason for the debacle that triggered the need to divest was the complex derivatives transactions that had gone horribly wrong. This constituted a major setback. The kind of crisis that can send a firm into a tailspin. We were made of sterner stuff.

I decided to deal with the issues at hand on two or three separate fronts in a step-by-step manner. First, I spoke to the CDR teams at banks we were dealing with and gave them two options. The first was that we could fully convert our debt into preferential shares and make part of the repayment by 2016 or 2017 at the market price of equity shares. They would then have the option of taking the equity or not doing so. The balance, I said, would be redeemed in 2018 or 2019 at a certain agreed upon price. In other words, we did some time discounting. The second option was that we would settle with banks that wanted payment in cash at 25 per cent of the value of the principal.

All the Indian banks, except State Bank of India, took the first option. They believed in us and agreed that the paramount objective of the methodology adopted should be the survival of a good and well-managed company that had a creditable track record, both in terms of what we were producing and how we had thus far managed our finances. Most foreign banks, barring ABN Amro and Deutsche Bank, chose the second option. Mind you, we were offering to repay only 25 per cent of the value of the principal amount. Nobody in India had, to the best of my knowledge, offered such a low price. I was a bit worried when I made the offer. Would they bite?

Despite our good image and track record, several cases had been filed against us and we were worried about reputational risk. We had to deal with a variety of exposures ranging from derivatives to cheque-bouncing! Fortunately, our businesses were generating adequate cash. To deal with the derivatives exposure we offered the two-part scheme I mentioned.

Some banks chose to take us to court, but we were able to argue convincingly in the court that it was not just us that had erred in performing our fiduciary due diligence on derivatives trading but that the bank too had not done its job. They did not warn us about the risks involved. In fact, several banks, especially some of the foreign banks, had actively encouraged our finance managers to invest in derivatives. Our lawyers were able to point to the fact that some banks had in fact violated the Reserve Bank of India's rules and had misled us in the process. The strength of our case forced some banks to approach us and negotiate their way out of what was by then recognized as a global phenomenon afflicting banks and firms. While J.P. Morgan chose to settle with us, ABN Amro held out, which forced us to launch a thorough investigation into our dealings with them. We found there were a lot of violations on their part of RBI rules and norms pertaining to derivatives. In dealing with this case we had to even hire a criminal lawyer and we built a strong case pertaining to cheating. They finally settled with us after a criminal prosecution was launched against the bank and some of its officers.

My second step, once we finished with crisis management, was to sign on to a CDR programme. I must mention that of all the people I spoke to and who helped me, one of the more professional bankers who educated me and advised me was Santosh B. Nayar, then Chief General Manager at the State Bank of India in Mumbai. He looked at our case, understood the seriousness of the problem, explained it to me and suggested that we enter into a CDR agreement with his bank. In March 2009, we signed on to CDR. The moment a company does that, all liabilities and payment obligations are frozen. This helped ease our cash position and the cash we had with us was adequate to carry on our normal business activity.

I cannot overemphasize the role of individuals in this entire saga. If one man got us into trouble, another helped us get out of it. Apart from SBI's Santosh Nayar, I must also acknowledge the help we got from Kalpesh Kikani of ICICI. Both trusted Wockhardt, knew we would right the wrong and come out of a bad situation and so stood by us. SBI and ICICI together supervised and helped implement the CDR process to its logical end.

We were able to redeem all our debts, repay every bank and clean up our accounts. Not only was ours an arguably unique case of a company coming successfully out of CDR, but we also managed to do so in the shortest possible time. When I look back at that entire episode what is heartening to note is that our financial troubles were not the result of wrong business decisions or faulty transactions, but merely of faulty financial management. The crisis did not hurt our core business in generics, development of NCEs, biotech research and product development, nor our manufacturing efficiency and distribution channels.

We divested some of our best assets and businesses to not just restore the financial health of the company but to also take it on a new growth path. In the process, we divested portions of our hospitals business. Ten of our seventeen hospitals, including our hospitals at Mulund and Bengaluru, were sold to Fortis. I sold our animal healthcare business to Vétoquinol, a French company, using the proceeds to pay off debts. I also sold our successful nutrition business to Danone, another French company. The philosophy was simple. Divest from non-core business to strengthen core business. I encapsulated this philosophy in the motto: 'More & More with Less & Less'.

The setbacks were limited to some of our business in France and Germany. Even there our business decisions were sound and extremely well thought out. But the external financial environment in the transatlantic economies was such that we also took a hit. In short, the financial risks we took did not hurt our core business activity in India and rest of the world. That in itself was a reward and proof of the soundness of our overall management approach.

Years later my present financial head, Manas Datta, told me that he had heard many in the financial sector make the point that Wockhardt was probably the only major Indian company to sacrifice its crown jewels to safeguard its core businesses.

∽

By 2013, our sales in the US market exceeded $500 million, with almost twenty-six products from our Chikalthana and Waluj facilities being sold there. We are down to $150 million today, as we are in the process of putting in place remedial measures to address all the concerns of the regulator in the US. For a company that many thought was on the brink of collapse, not only did we bounce back in the US market but we also chose to spend 12 per cent of our consolidated turnover on R&D and now have an impressive line-up of five NCE candidates in the antibiotics business, all receiving the QIDP status, making Wockhardt the only company in the world to achieve this for five candidates. To top it all, we are now getting into expensive clinical trials for our antibiotics drug candidates and will be investing in a big way there— again the only company to do so.

In our core business, I have never shied away from uncharted waters. I can take measured risks there, think long term and have the willingness to wait for results. I have never been hungry for quick, risk-adjusted returns on businesses.

In the last three years (2013–16), we lost almost $350 million in business in the US—a market that offers something like a 60 per cent margin. However, a closer look at our balance sheet will show that our net worth has remained the same during the three years. At its worst, the business was down only by some $10 million. We were able to pay close to $60 million as dividend. Our cash generation to earnings before interest, taxes, depreciation and amortization (EBITDA) is presently one of the highest in the Indian pharma industry. Generally, 65 per cent of the EBITDA contributes to cash generation, but for us it is over 75 per cent, even today. This only goes to show our sound profitability.

Because there was nothing wrong intrinsically with our business, we could bounce back. In 2006, our turnover was ₹5 billion, by 2016 it was over ₹40 billion. An eightfold increase, despite the financial crisis and the CDR process. The point to note is that most of our businesses abroad continue to do well. All in all, if four out of five deals abroad worked well then it is not a bad score for the company. Which in a sense means we did not misread the market and were right in our approach.

If there was any positive spin-off from the derivatives transactions episode, it was that I began to devote more time to Wockhardt's financial management. In 2014 I recruited the highly talented Manas Datta as the head of finance. Since his taking charge we have fine-tuned our governance practices, which means that all decisions are put before the board followed by serious deliberations at the board level.

On derivatives, for instance, we approached the board and it approved our motion that the company will not enter into any derivatives transactions. Instead, for any decision that involves taking a forward cover, the chairman, managing director and the chief financial officer (CFO) will have to put it all in writing with the three signing on it. In other words, there has to be utmost discipline in these matters.

In my communication to our investors and shareholders, I had committed in my letter in the annual report of 2008 that 'circumstances are the best teachers' and said that 'as a deft organization, Wockhardt will be more focused in managing its cash flows and working capital efficiently and will initiate better inventory and cost management.'

Risk is intrinsic to business in a world of uncertainty. However, when one realizes that in one area of business the company has been exposed to unacceptably high risk, all effort must be made to de-risk on all other fronts till the problem at hand has been adequately addressed. So, when we became exposed to the derivatives risk, we opted for CDR to quickly restore the company's overall financial health. We shut shop on some fronts, like some of our hospitals, and went slow on others, like new product launches. These decisions hurt specific segments of the company, but helped the overall situation and enabled us to get out of CDR quickly.

I used to give the example of Tata's Nano to some of my colleagues as an instance of how not to deal with risk. Launching a revolutionary new product like a 'people's car' that would be an entry-level small car in a rapidly evolving automobile market was itself a fantastic idea fraught with huge risk. To then locate it in a state like West Bengal, given its unpredictable, high-risk political environment was to multiply rather than reduce the risk. Nano ought to have been launched from Gujarat, Maharashtra and Tamil Nadu. When one takes a big risk on one front, one must de-risk as much as possible on all other fronts.

⚮

In 2013, we faced yet another challenge. Some issues pertaining to regulatory compliance came up and warning letters were issued by the USFDA. Our exports to the US dropped sharply, declining by as much as 49 per cent within the year. Our focus, quite rightly, shifted to regulatory compliance and to addressing the concerns raised by the USFDA and the authorities in the UK. For instance, we expanded our quality team by nearly 40 per cent and put senior management in charge of quality. We had to invest time and effort in training as automation increased. The results were encouraging as the good manufacturing practice (GMP) certification from the UK's Medicines and Healthcare Products Regulatory Agency was restored for our

Chikalthana and Kadaiya facilities and we commenced our supplies to the UK. Once again, our core business strength helped us to get on top of the situation.

By 2014–15, Wockhardt's UK business grew by 46 per cent and we filed fourteen ANDAs with the USFDA and launched forty-two new products in India. The domestic business grew by as much as 24 per cent. To top it all, it turned out to be a milestone year for us in our NCE journey. Two of our new antiinfective drugs under development, WCK 771 and WCK 2349, were recognized as breakthrough discoveries in the antibiotics space by the USFDA. They received the coveted QIDP status, which paves the way for fast-track review by the regulator, enabling an early launch when cleared.

What made the moment even more special for us at Wockhardt was that this was the first instance of an Indian pharmaceutical company receiving the QIDP status. In fact, by May 2015, one more product under development, WCK 4873, was also granted the QIDP status, making Wockhardt the first pharmaceutical company in the world to get this status for three breakthrough drugs under development. As you know, the number is up to five today. The credit should naturally go to the scientific resource of the company.

As you can see, we have been preparing for our next orbital shift. We are ready to become an NCE-led global pharmaceutical company. If going global took us into one orbit, becoming an NCE-led firm will take us into the next orbit. Today, the Wockhardt family of over ten thousand comprises people of twenty-seven nationalities, and the company has a physical presence across geographies as wide-ranging as the US, the UK, Ireland, Mexico and Russia, among others. It has manufacturing and research facilities in India, the US and the UK, and a manufacturing facility in Ireland. Today, over 60 per cent of our global revenues come from our international business.

Antibiotics is the future and I have little doubt about this. All we need to do is look at the growing bacterial resistance to drugs, a result of the rampant overuse and misuse of antibiotics. Most of the regularly used antibiotics such as azithromycin, cephalosporin, piperacillin/tazobactam and clarithromycin have attained resistance of up to 15 to 20 per cent in the regulated markets and much more in emerging markets. Pharmaceutical companies clearly have their work cut out for them, and we want to lead the way.

My association with the Khorakiwalas goes back to the early 1960s. At that time, I met Habil's father, Fakhruddin Khorakiwala, many times, but essentially at the Basic Chemicals Export Promotion Council's meetings at Jhansi Castle near the Oval. We were all trying to promote exports and I clearly remember the gentleman who ran it at that time was a Sitaram. The Khorakiwalas ran a general store called Akbarallys at Flora Fountain. They also had a small pharma unit at Worli called Worli Chemicals. The name was later changed to Wockhardt. It was only through Habil's father that I got to know Habil, who in the late 1960s created Wockhardt. He was a young man then, but highly motivated to do well in the pharma world, which I am proud to say he has.

In the early 1970s, the main products of Wockhardt were Proxyvon and a family of drugs based on this. They became the foundation of Wockhardt, which, at that time, was not manufacturing raw materials. In the late 1970s, I told Habil that he should go into the manufacture of active ingredients and I clearly remember him telling me that he did not know anything about this. I suggested to him, at the time, that he manufacture the actives that Wockhardt used and I would help him. I did help and, in due course, Wockhardt took up the manufacture of dextropropoxyphene. Habil was quick to learn and Wockhardt soon became one of India's leading API producers.

Habil took the company to great heights, not only in the Indian market but also internationally, in particular, to the regulated markets of Europe, the UK and the US. His achievements in the Indian pharmaceutical industry over the years have been outstanding. He has outdone his late father and is regarded, today, as a stalwart of the Indian pharma industry.

Apart from the above and the close association we have, I would like to say something about his personal life and family. His wife, Nafisa, is a great philanthropist, as also are his three children. They run major hospitals in India. Habil himself is very much involved nowadays in research and development, and hopefully some of the products developed will be acclaimed internationally. Time has not changed him. At the age of seventy-five, he is physically and mentally as young as he was in his earlier days. Apart from being very intelligent, Habil has always had a very pleasant and cheerful attitude to life. He has a deep sense of friendship, warmth and humour. He cares for his friends and associates and is appreciated by all who know him. Hopefully, Habil will go on to score a century at the wicket of life and Wockhardt, under the Khorakiwalas, will go on to greater heights. I wish him and his family all the very best in the years ahead.

**Yusuf Hamied**, Chairman, Cipla

## Chapter 8

# Learning by Doing

*For the things we have to learn before we can do them,
we learn by doing them.*

—Aristotle

Failure is the beginning of learning. I am glad that this was a lesson I learnt early in life. My father would always reassure me that making a mistake was never wrong, but making the same mistake again was foolish. One should learn from one's mistakes but never be afraid of making them, he would say. When you fail to secure the result you seek, when you fail to meet the goal you pursue, you sit back and ask: why did I fail? With each such failure in my business plans I learnt important lessons. Lessons about managing people. Lessons about managing money. Managing time. Lessons about educating oneself on concepts, on ideas relevant for one's business. Some of these lessons are learnt by listening, reading, talking. But the most enduring lessons are learnt by doing.

I have rarely walked the beaten path. I have always been driven by the intense desire to be different, to do something new, or to do familiar things differently. Differentiation, I have always believed, is the key to success. It forces you to tread new paths. Anyone can walk on a path already made. It takes courage to walk on untrodden ground with the firm conviction that others will follow and a path will be made in the process.

I have often been asked why I am so obsessed with doing things differently. Such questions always place the seeds of doubt in one's mind. Am I doing things differently for the sake of doing so? Is this an obsession? A luxury one cannot afford in a highly competitive business?

I have been overcome by such self-doubt every now and then. More often than not I set such doubts aside and keep doing what I am doing. Only once in a while have I stepped back and played it safe to reassure those around me who worry about my offbeat approach to opportunities and challenges. One can be in business doing what everyone else is doing. I am not made that way. I believe that the future of Wockhardt lies in being different.

However, I must enter a word of caution. Even as one treads the unknown path, in business one must always subject oneself to a reality check. Do the results support your decisions? Have you been vindicated by the outcome? Does the data back your decision? I never impose my views on others till I am sure that the facts are on my side. Once I am confident that things have worked out the way I would have liked them to, I communicate my thinking to my colleagues so that they know my thought process and come to learn from it.

The process of the evolution of my thinking is that I first act on my instincts and beliefs; then, I evaluate my decisions against what I am able to achieve; and, finally I communicate all this to my colleagues.

The moment you communicate your thought process to your colleagues you take on a new burden. The burden of living with the consequences of their following your example! A leader who believes in taking risks must have great tolerance for colleagues also taking risks and making mistakes.

Risk-taking in business is not like playing Russian roulette. One has to take what I would call 'measured risks'. This implies constant monitoring of what one does and a willingness to correct oneself when a mistake is made. Of course, this also implies knowing that a mistake has been made, which is where data analysis and data monitoring come in. Fact-checking is the other side of the coin of risk-taking.

Business education is not just about learning from other people's successes but also, perhaps more importantly, learning from their mistakes. Books on management theory and practice are useful and one must read them, but most of them represent history. Rarely do they tell you what lies ahead. In any case, everybody has access to this published knowledge. One must have a healthy respect for that knowledge, not a blind respect for it. The key to success in business lies in one's ability to pick up knowledge that is relevant from the experience of others and then chart one's own path into the future, not being constrained by that knowledge but merely informed by it.

When one is in a leadership position in industry one tends to talk only about one's successes, but one must remember that others would also like to learn from one's failures. The process of learning entails learning about what contributes to success and failure. One should never be shy or ashamed of imitating the success of others. That is not being a copycat. Following other people's good practices is learning, not copying. One must imbibe all that is good.

So, while on the one hand you should not be afraid to do things differently, on the other hand, if somebody is doing something right and you know that it will be successful, then go ahead and do it yourself.

What reading and familiarity with existing knowledge give one is depth of understanding. That has to be matched with one's self-confidence, which enables one to do things differently. This idea was put to me in the profoundest of ways by a Hindustani classical vocalist, Sunita Bhuyan, who explained to me that a good singer is one who masters the art through repeated practise but has the ability to innovate when performing. The ability to innovate comes only from firm grounding in the traditional. 'Depth gives flexibility', she summed up. Depth in understanding music is important because the deeper your understanding of a raga the greater is your ability to innovate. It was the most important lesson in business practice that I have ever received. To be able to do things differently, one must be a master in doing them conventionally.

∽

From a fairly early stage in the growth of Wockhardt I had the aspiration to go global. Perhaps it was the sea in Mumbai that always beckoned me. Perhaps it was my experience as a student at Purdue. Perhaps it was the confidence I gained when I spent thirteen weeks at Harvard. But the desire to go global was there and became only more compelling. However, I was cautious enough to recognize that one must always maintain a balance between the known and the unknown. How does one become a global company if one's entire experience has been local? What were my knowns? Our products, our people, our technology. What were my unknowns? The market abroad and the work ethic abroad. So, I decided I should first acquire a going concern that was doing reasonably well in a country like Britain. We Indians feel more comfortable in the UK.

I had no clue how to negotiate an acquisition abroad. So we hired someone who could help us learn. It took us some time to negotiate satisfactory terms. It was not a large firm. We invested £2 million. Our first problem arose when the existing management team left the company. They were not willing to work with us. We had to hire a new managing director. I found a Dutch gentleman, living in the UK, who had worked for Upjohn, a US firm based in Michigan. However, he did not meet our expectations and the company continued to bleed. For me it was a dispiriting experience. But I refused to lose faith or confidence in myself. I decided to change the leader and see if a new managing director would make a difference. If I had been risk-averse,

I would have perhaps hired an Englishman with local exposure and experience. My experience with the Dutch manager convinced me that what I needed was a person who understood our company and me as well as the terrain in which he was operating. So I looked for someone who had worked with us.

We had a finance director at Wockhardt, V. Rajan, who chose to go abroad to seek global exposure and experience. He had worked in Nigeria for some time and had then moved to Indonesia. I tracked him down and invited him to return home with the offer of an eventual move to London. I wanted him to first get up to speed on where we were and intended to be, before packing him off to the UK.

Rajan was a good financial manager and I wanted to figure out why the UK operation was not coming out of the red. When we met and spoke I realized that Rajan and I were on the same wavelength. He understood me and my objectives and his approach to human management gelled very well with our management culture. So, instead of offering him just the finance portfolio I appointed him as our managing director in the UK. It had by then occurred to me that the problem with the Dutch manager was that he was just a manager. I needed someone with entrepreneurial skills capable of turning a company in the red around. Rajan had worked in a difficult place like Nigeria and had then moved to a very different environment in Indonesia. He was not just a good financial manager, but he also had the skills required to deal with diverse cultures.

Rajan came up with out-of-the-box solutions and was able to deliver results within months.

My first learning from this experience was that past experience is no basis for judging a person's future performance. The Dutch manager had excellent managerial credentials. He had domain knowledge. But he was unable to deliver. Rajan's domain knowledge was in finance, but his global exposure taught him to deal with new environments. It was not his résumé or his domain knowledge that made the difference, but his soft skills, his ability to understand our corporate objectives and his ability to work with a completely new set of people from a very different country and culture. I realized that what we needed in our second line of leadership was managers who not only understood my way of thinking but had a bit of the entrepreneur in them.

Since my mind was set on taking Wockhardt to the world I had to know how I would manage our firms outside India. I realized that hiring someone who had worked at a multinational and knew the foreign territory well was neither sufficient nor necessary. I needed a person who first understood my company and me. He would also have to have the soft skills that would enable him to handle new environments. At the highest management levels of a company one does not need people with only domain knowledge. Such qualified persons are best kept at the operational level, which is a rung below. At the top one needs people who can deal with people. Top management is about people management—people within the firm and people one must deal with outside the firm.

Management, I have come to believe, is more an art than a science. The first lesson I learnt from my own experience in doing business was that managing a business is first and foremost about understanding people and knowing how to deal with different kinds of people. The second most important qualification for top management is competence in the management of finance. Rajan knew how to manage money and people. A successful entrepreneur must have these two abilities—managing people and finance. The rest is secondary. One need not know much about manufacturing and marketing. There are professionals who can handle that.

❧

I learnt my second important lesson—the value of seeking external and impartial advice, even if one felt one had all the answers—when we acquired Merind in February 1998. It was originally a Merck company that had later been acquired by the Tatas. Merind had an impressive pedigree. It was a joint venture company between Merck Sharp & Dohme or Merck & Co, USA, and Tata Sons. Later, Merck & Co exited and it became a Tata company. It had a facility at Tardeo in Mumbai that was later shifted to Bhandup, also in Mumbai. It manufactured antibiotics, corticosteroids, antihypertensives, antihistamines and even vitamin B-12 from the very basic stage. In fact, it was the second company in the world to make vitamin B-12.

Around 1996, Ratan Tata decided to sell Merind. A managing director was given the responsibility of carrying out the sale. But, as we found out, the managing director seemed happy to run his little empire and showed no interest in finding a buyer for his company! I was aware of Ratan's plans, so we approached him through an intermediary, Nimesh Kampani, and made an offer. We had done thorough due diligence and knew everything we needed to know about the company. My technical and financial teams were not allowed to visit the premises because the managing director felt this would create concerns within his team. We were allowed to examine only the database that was provided to us. I didn't mind because as Merind was originally a Merck facility and then a Tata facility, I was reasonably confident that it would be in good condition. My legal, technical and financial teams pored over the data and gave me the go-ahead.

The rule at the time required that we buy at least 20 per cent of the equity. The Tatas had 51 per cent ownership in the company. They quoted a price that required us to buy only 20 per cent from the public. We then proposed to them that we would be willing to acquire 100 per cent of the shares, to be fair to all shareholders, but at a lower price. They agreed. I valued Tata's decision as it was fair to all shareholders.

Merind was a major acquisition. As it was almost half the size of Wockhardt, we were suddenly going to expand with that one acquisition. The challenge for me was integrating my existing facilities and staff with the newly acquired entity.

I asked McKinsey&Co. to advise me on integrating the two companies and, more importantly, the two management teams. The advantage of hiring a consultant, that too a globally experienced firm, was that we were able to reduce the cost of acquisition and integration.

I was impressed by the talent and work ethic of the McKinsey staff. They drew on their global talent pool at every stage to bring in knowledge of issues from around the world. McKinsey's consultants studied both companies and advised me against a hurried integration. There would be a clash of cultures, they warned me. Ours was an entrepreneur-created and driven company, while Merind had started as a multinational and was then managed by a large entity like the Tatas.

I invited McKinsey to chart out a roadmap and guide us through the process. They drew up tight timelines and goals and made them clear to the top management of both Merind and Wockhardt. But I told my staff to carefully study everything that McKinsey was saying and doing so that in future we would be able to manage an acquisition on our own, without hiring an outside consultant. I was happy that my colleagues and the consultants worked very well together and we internalized all the learnings. As a result, for the next two decades I did not have to hire any outside consultant even as we kept acquiring companies both in India and abroad.

∽

Over the years, we have established a fairly good system of measuring performance. Among the management experts who helped me with the process was my good friend the late B.L. Maheshwari. I recall reading an article about him in the Mumbai-based magazine, *Blitz*, which said he was perhaps the highest paid management consultant in India at the time, charging the princely fee of ₹3,000 per day. In the early

1980s, that would have been the monthly salary of many managers.

I approached Maheshwari at the time and invited him to help us streamline our management systems. He introduced me to new concepts of performance assessment and appraisal that we quickly implemented for all managers. He taught us how to set measurable goals in quantitative terms and also how to define what was not quantifiable in qualitative terms. Initially, the focus of our MBO approach was in mainline business management in areas such as corporate oversight, finance, HR, marketing and supply chain management.

However, over time, as the research and science base of the company increased and we began to employ more and more scientists, we had to define new ways in which to think about MBO. I also realized that it was necessary to train our business managers so they would be better able to deal with scientists. The idea that 'thinking' is also 'doing' and that 'studying' can be an economically productive activity for a company, is new to managers who have never worked with and managed scientists and researchers.

Unlike in manufacturing and marketing, in research there are far too many uncertainties and unknowns. One is inventing something that did not exist earlier. Scientists work in the realm of ideas and create material outcomes from their thinking. That is the pharmaceutical business. An idea gets translated into a drug that makes a physical difference to living beings. Business managers also deal with ideas, but most often they use known knowledge to deal with a range of anticipatable situations to achieve planned objectives. A scientist uses known knowledge to create new knowledge and thereby make the unknown or unanticipated a material reality.

Given that business managers and scientists have not just different objectives, but different ways of defining objectives and the path to the realization of those objectives, one cannot be too conservative in running a research- and science-based pharmaceutical company. I have always found the challenge of dealing with people who make greater use of the right side of the brain and those who make greater use of the left side a fascinating learning experience.

Finally, Maheshwari taught me one more thing about setting objectives. He would say, if you are doing a hundred today, then saying that you will do a hundred and two next year is no way of defining an objective. The growth from a hundred to a hundred and two is a natural process. It does not require managerial leadership and planning and strategy. If, however, you say that you will do a hundred and twenty, then that requires managerial leadership and intervention. MBO has to focus on that.

Learning by doing is intrinsic to both doing business and to doing research. The one difference though is that in business you cannot really afford to fail repeatedly. In research, the definition of failure is itself vague. One learns something new from every scientific experiment. There is addition to knowledge. When one conducts an experiment one may fail to achieve the expected results, but one never fails to learn and build on that. In science, learning by doing is a lifelong endeavour, even when there are no immediate rewards. Business demands rewards, not just in this lifetime, but in this year. Indeed, in this quarter!

I do not recall my first encounter with Habil, since the association has been long—stretching over twenty-five years. It must have been at an industry association or a pharma conference forum. I have known Habil as a passionate businessman with a far-sighted vision. Wockhardt is a leader in the pharma business, and Habil has been successful in registering local presence in host markets, including a string of acquisitions. Many of his peers stopped short with export-led distribution agreements. This certainly fast-tracked Wockhardt's ascendancy in select markets. Habil is a risk-taker but not reckless in any way. His investments in drug discovery, focused on antibiotics/antibacterials, are testimony to his vision and risk-taking capacity.

Habil has great control over his emotions and is able to remain unfazed in very difficult circumstances. This is a great leadership trait as it inhibits panic reaction and defuses tension. He is a very warm-hearted person, who shows care and understanding. He is charismatic in his own style.

He is committed to CSR from much before it was made mandatory for the corporate sector by the government. He cares for people and is generous. In his own lifestyle, he is understated and so is his family.

My relationship has changed from casual exchanges at industry meetings of the IDMA, OPPI, the IPA, and FICCI etc., or deliberations regarding policy framework for the pharma industry to a relationship of trust, warmth, understanding and high professional respect. When my decision to leave Ranbaxy in 2004 was made known, I recall vividly how Habil flew down to Delhi to meet and request me to join the Wockhardt board and even offered the privilege of being co-chairman of the company. He outlined a partnership model of value creation also. I was greatly touched by his sincerity, thoughtfulness and the generous offer to be part of Wockhardt's growth journey. While I could not join Wockhardt in 2004, our association became stronger till Habil finally persuaded me to join the board, eight years later. In those eight years, our professional friendship grew.

My earlier impressions of Habil have changed, as I find him more compassionate and a person who gives a lot to the society. Also, his management style reinforces my distant impressions where he remains the cord which binds the company together. Wockhardt has had ongoing debt and regulatory issues over the last five years, which have impacted its growth journey and overall standing. Through all this, Habil has stood tall and unflinching. His personal value system is one that commands respect.

**Davinder Singh Brar**, Chairman, GVK Bio

# Chapter 9

# Firm and the Family

*If a country is to be corruption-free and become a nation of beautiful minds, I strongly feel there are three key societal members who can make a difference. They are the father, the mother and the teacher.*

—A.P.J. Abdul Kalam

*I* grew up in a family that did business. In my grandfather's time, it was more like a joint family. He was the unquestioned head. However, he understood business and allowed his children to try their hand at doing their own thing. That was true for my generation too. Early in our business career my siblings and I went our own way in business. My grandfather and his brother were the pioneers, but my father was entrepreneurial too. His decision, early in life, to leave the security of our family, social and business environment in Mumbai to try his hand at business in distant Kolkata was a sign of that desire to strike out on his own. I learnt an important lesson from that episode in my father's life. I allowed each of my three children to first do their own thing before encouraging them to return to the fold, as it were.

*Habil Khorakiwala with the much-loved and admired*
*former President A.P.J. Abdul Kalam*

My eldest, Huzaifa, studied commerce at the graduate level and earned a Master's in Business Management from the Yale University Management School in the US. On completing his studies, he was enamoured by IT-enabled businesses and started a digital travel company with an online ticketing system. I encouraged him to do something on his own so that he would get a feel of doing business away from the comfort of the family. He did that for a while and then decided to join Wockhardt, taking charge of the veterinary business and the work of the Wockhardt Foundation.

Murtaza went into medicine, enrolling for an MBBS degree. I strongly encouraged him to do so. He too went to the US to acquire a Master's in Business Administration from the University of Illinois. He too was enamoured by IT like so many young persons of his generation. That was the rage at the time and many Indian companies were making their global mark in software development and IT-enabled services.

I had only one word of advice for him, as I did later for Zahabiya also. I advised them to find a business partner who would be willing to invest in whatever they wanted to do. That was a way of ensuring that someone else felt the business venture was worth investing in. It was a kind of risk management that forced them to run their ideas past their peers and see if there would be any takers.

I allowed all my children to do what they liked, even though what they attempted was entirely different from the business we are in. I believed that when they succeed, it would boost their confidence and teach them how to establish a new business on their own. On the other hand, if they failed, they would also learn lessons on why their venture failed. In either case, they would go through the entire process that an entrepreneur goes through, dealing with various ups and downs on the way. That in itself is a great lesson learnt.

Murtaza found a friend who was willing to partner with him and they launched their company in the US itself. I was a bit anxious about the prospects of his IT venture and encouraged him to return home. He wanted to live abroad for a while longer, especially after he got married. So I encouraged him to move to England and manage Wallis Laboratories.

Zahabiya did part of her schooling at Aiglon in Switzerland and went on to study psychology at New York University. A part of that period was spent at a campus in Florence. She too chose to start her own company, with a friend. It was into making bubble drinks. She then earned a degree in business management from the Indian School of Business, spending part of her course time in Barcelona.

Each of my children had a grounding in India and acquired reasonable global exposure. Their education helped broaden their vision. It was only fair that I offered the space for their further growth without imposing any conditions or constraints.

Each spent a few years pursuing their individual interests. When they were on their own my approach was simple—if you succeed fine;

*Habil Khorakiwala's mother listening intently to his father*

*Habil Khorakiwala sharing a joke with wife Nafisa*

*Habil Khorakiwala's father addressing the family during a get-together*

*Habil Khorakiwala playing cricket at the family farmhouse*

if you fail, learn from the experience. The important thing was that they tried their hand at doing what they wanted to, before returning to the fold and having to do what they were required to. None of them could complain that their parents prevented them from doing what they wanted to!

Everyone has individual aspirations that a family cannot always cater to. But the family members should be allowed to pursue those aspirations before returning to devote their time and energy to the family business.

As a consequence, their generation has a broader vision and much more self-confidence than mine did. In time, the three have taken their respective places within the larger Wockhardt family—Huzaifa initially handled the veterinary business and he now oversees the work of the Wockhardt Foundation, something that he is deeply interested in. He has made a mark for himself and for Wockhardt in the promotion of CSR. Having studied medicine and given his skills as a manager, Murtaza has been able to take charge of the core business, managing both the Indian and global manufacturing and marketing operations.

We had an ongoing relationship with Harvard Medical International—now rechristened as Partners Medical International. Zahabiya had a great opportunity to interact with the Partners team in Boston and with the management of various hospitals. She has carved her niche in managing our hospital business. She is very passionate about what she does and wants to create an institution of excellence in healthcare that has the potential to create new landmarks in clinical care.

It was providential that each of my children had a different interest and willingly took up different responsibilities. There was no competition among them nor any sense of jealousy or that one wanted to do what another was doing. Huzaifa opted to take charge of the Wockhardt Foundation and has been deeply engaged in its growing and highly innovative activities. The Foundation has won many awards and has been recognized for its deep commitment to the work it is doing and the very innovative nature of that work, which impacts three milllion lives every year.

I remember counselling Murtaza on his choices regarding further education around the time he completed the twelfth standard. I advised him that if he wanted to study in India (which was his choice at that time), then there were two streams of good quality education— engineering and medicine. Being in pharmaceuticals and healthcare, I obviously suggested it made more sense for him to pursue medicine, which he considered very seriously and thus was born the first medical doctor in our family. Today, looking back, I feel that was the right decision for him, given how it shaped his career and involvement at Wockhardt.

After dabbling as an entrepreneur for over a year in his IT start-up in the US, Murtaza seemed to be reflecting on his choices for his career and future. It was around that time that I flew to the US to spend some time with him to help provide a clear perspective on being involved with Wockhardt in the UK and how it would impact and enrich his life. This eventually resulted in him moving to the UK to handle our operations there. I do believe, though, that his experience in the IT start-up provided him with valuable lessons both in business and technology, which were of use to him later at Wockhardt.

After taking charge as managing director of our pharmaceuticals and biotechnology business in 2009, Murtaza has been at my side as a source of great support. His medical and management training background enabled him to get a good grasp of the issues in handling the overall business responsibility. Over the years Murtaza has shown immense growth, maturity and perseverance in good and serious times. I have given him tough challenges to handle to make sure that he emerges from those experiences stronger and richer. As a father, I feel proud of his accomplishments, as indeed of those of my other children, Huzaifa and Zahabiya. They have injected new energy into each of the initiatives they handle.

*Habil Khorakiwala at his home 'Casa Khorakiwala' with family and friends*

Nafisa has played an important role both as a mother and a mentor to our children. When we got married she was not really interested in business or what I was doing at work. Her world was the family and she took great care in the upbringing of the children. Through their school years she was always there for them. She ensured that she instilled good values in them, and was quite strict, with explicit 'Dos and Don'ts'. It was only when she accompanied me to Harvard, when I enrolled for the Advanced Management Programme, that she began to get an exposure to the world of business. Harvard has a programme for participants' spouses in the last of the programme's thirteen weeks. This involves some lectures and an introduction to some case studies. Nafisa's interest in and empathy for what I was doing back home suddenly increased. After the programme she told me that for the first time she realized the complexities and issues involved in doing business. Once our children finished school, Nafisa became actively involved with the Wockhardt Foundation.

Both Nafisa and I feel proud that each of our three children have found their niche within the larger Wockhardt family and are making their mark in their areas of responsibility. I am now confident that even without me around, they can take Wockhardt to greater heights. All this has meant that I have a limited role in the daily management. My primary focus now is to create the Wockhardt of tomorrow. We are in the process of transforming Wockhardt into a global research-based organization developing new and innovative medicines for unmet medical needs. I find this journey enormously exciting and challenging. It keeps my adrenaline flowing and this may possibly be one of the best periods in my life. We are dreaming and doing successfully that which no other company from India has dared.

∽

An important principle that Nafisa and I have adhered to is 'fairness'— that we treat our three children as equals in all business-related matters. First and foremost that means no gender discrimination. Zahabiya gets the same remuneration for her work as Huzaifa and Murtaza do. They have equal pay and equal inheritance of wealth.

*Habil Khorakiwala and Nafisa with their three children—Murtaza,
Zahabiya and Huzaifa (from left to right)*

My most important corporate objective in dealing with my three
children has been to avoid any basis for sibling rivalry or conflict. So

many Indian business families have been hurt by this. Till 1991, the Licence-Permit-Quota Raj played its role in stunting the growth of the Indian corporate sector, forcing companies to operate at suboptimal levels of capacity and size. However, after 1991, family disputes, sibling rivalries and the subdivision of properties by large business families contributed to the continuation of such suboptimality and the inability of many firms to exploit scale economies and emerge as large global players.

So, I would say the first principle of successful family management in business is to ensure fairness in the treatment of the next generation. As a mother, Nafisa may have a soft corner for one or the other child just as I, as a father, have a soft corner for our only daughter, the youngest of the three. But as the chairman of the company, I have no soft corners and have tried my best to institutionalize the relationship between the chairman and family directors.

Second, I insist that all my children be physically present in crucial meetings when important decisions are taken so as to understand the process through observation. I tell them, 'just be there and observe'. They attend many meetings and learn by observation. They are always free to express their views, in fact, they do! However, there is great learning in mere observation. That is a part of the ongoing process of mentoring.

Having ensured fairness and enforced participation through observation, the next step is of empowerment. Once I handed over the biotech/pharma business to Murtaza, the Foundation to Huzaifa and the hospitals to Zahabiya, I fully empowered them. Once Zahabiya came to me and said that she was scared by the amount of trust I had reposed in her and her judgement.

I have made it a point not to review their performance too closely. It was a deliberate policy decision on my part. When one begins a detailed post-facto scrutiny of decisions taken, those who made the decisions become not only defensive but also risk-averse. It is human nature to want approval and seek approbation. In business, it is important to understand that mistakes are not wrong. They are just lessons for the future. Sometimes I have found their judgement to be better than mine. That has reinforced my belief that one must give one's children the space to grow, to differ, to learn and, in turn, help me learn.

*Murtaza Khorakiwala receiving the Zee Family Legacy Business Award instituted by the Essel group from former President Pranab Mukherjee.*
*Also on stage are Prime Minister Narendra Modi and the chairman of Essel Group, Subhash Chandra*

There is a huge difference between guiding someone and evaluating the person. In a family business, a family elder can and must guide younger members. But their evaluation has to be based on self-criticism and peer review. My objective has always been that my children grow to be good leaders and not followers. Excessive direction and advice saps initiative and will never allow one to be a good leader and a successful entrepreneur.

There is a difference between how I evaluate the work of a senior manager versus that of a family director. A senior manager is involved in decision-making, but in the final analysis his or her performance is evaluated on the basis of how well those decisions have been implemented. In grooming my children as future business leaders I had to help them grow as risk-takers and leaders and not just as good managers. It is not enough if they do a good job in implementing the board's decisions. They must have the ability to offer leadership to the board, take risks, take difficult decisions and grow the business.

Historical experience shows that a business organization has to survive at least two to three generational transitions for it to grow from being a good company to a great company. Some of the biggest US multinationals like IBM, GE and Ford had to survive three generations to go from good to great. Any organization or business can become a great organization and sustain itself over a long period of time if it is able to constantly generate good leadership. My ambition is that at some point Wockhardt grows from being good, which I believe it is, to becoming great. That is the task for the next generation. That has been my message to my children and the larger family.

∽

Wockhardt's initial growth was during the 1980s and 1990s when India was replete with reports of business families breaking up. Messy inheritance processes, sibling rivalries, complicated family relationships, varying levels of interest and competence in handling the family business among the heirs and a variety of other factors contributed to this. One sad consequence of all this for the country as a whole has been that instead of well-functioning Indian companies growing in size and becoming global players, they were divided and subdivided and their scales of operation became smaller rather than bigger.

Some of our pioneering business families who could have built global multinationals of reckoning have been held back by family disputes and the partitioning of assets. This is a pity because around the

*Habil Khorakiwala on a cruise with wife and friends.*
*From left: Baldev and Usha Arora, Nafisa, Habil, Kiran and Vijay Jalan*

*Habil Khorakiwala with Nafisa and cousin Shabbir and his wife Sherebanu*

*Habil Khorakiwala with Nafisa and friends at New Zealand's Glacier Valley Walk.*
*From left: Habil, Nafisa, Rajan and Usha Sanklecha, and*
*Shirley and Vijay Lazarus*

*Habil Khorakiwala with his brother Hunaid and his wife Shirin*

*Habil Khorakiwala at the Bhiwandi farm with brother Taizoon and his family*

*Habil Khorakiwala with Harsh Goenka and his wife Mala*

*Habil Khorakiwala greeting Nana Chudasama and his wife Munira*

*At the breathtaking setting of the Pangong Lake in Ladakh. From left:
Rashida Khorakiwala, Vijay Jalan, Nafisa, Habil Khorakiwala,
Baldev Arora and Uma Rao*

world—from the US to Japan, from Germany to South Korea—family-controlled businesses have created some of the biggest multinationals. It is the recognition of the fact that Indian business development has been hurt by family differences that has encouraged many of the more modern and liberal-minded business leaders to find concrete solutions to this enduring problem.

There is now a growing awareness among heads of family businesses that they should in fact have more structured methods and systems for the management and growth of their business, wealth and assets. A range of issues come up in the management of a family business. First, there are interpersonal issues—the father–son relationship, sibling rivalry, the role of the in-laws, gender relations, and so on. Second, there are issues pertaining to compensation and role. Third, there are issues around individual ambitions, skills, roles and responsibilities. Fourth are the issues related to the relationship between the family and professional managers. Finally, there are issues pertaining to succession planning.

I was fortunate in that there was no such bickering and break-ups in our family. Members of each generation found a way of doing their own thing, as it were. When I took charge of Wockhardt, I was pretty much on my own. My cousin Juzer was part of Wockhardt for some time and then went on to manage his own business. So the issue of generational transitions and the division of business was handled relatively smoothly across generations.

With Wockhardt we not only went public at home and abroad, but we also became a global company with varied business interests. I first had to find a way to get each of my children involved in the company. The company needed their talent and I was keen that they should step in. Once I ensured that, both Nafisa and I felt we should ensure the smooth functioning of the family and planned transitions across various businesses and activities. Moreover, observing the mayhem in Indian family businesses in the 1990s and after, I also felt we should have a proper structure and codes of conduct to carry our business forward.

I found that a new discipline had emerged in the field of business management focused on family businesses. The more progressive business families were adopting charters and constitutions and laying the rules of doing business for all family members. I decided that we should have a family charter, a formal system of interaction within the family, a transparent and rational methodology for the sharing and distribution of wealth and profit and so on.

In 2012, I approached two institutions that I knew were working in these areas and had the requisite experience and expertise. I felt confident that they would guide me and find a way of formalizing my thinking. I knew the leadership at Ernst & Young, India. I also approached Berjis Desai at the law firm J. Sagar Associates (JSA). I did think of other law firms but settled on JSA because I knew Berjis well and he knew us well. That was important for me.

In a matter like this the consultant must not only know the family, but must be able to appreciate the family's value system and philosophy. Without that empathy and understanding, no consultant can come up with sound advice. I was happy with the kind of advice I got from both E&Y and Berjis. I told them I had three principle objectives—whatever we put in place must be regarded by all as a fair system; second, it should leave no space for any misinterpretation, misunderstanding and conflict of interest; finally, it should stand the test of time.

It took us two years to arrive at a constitution because the existing templates that I found were inadequate for the purpose and objectives that I had in mind. We had to devote considerable time to discussing a variety of issues in great detail first within the family and then with the consultants. I did not want to rush into a half-baked solution. Any family governance system must last beyond a generation and must ensure long-term survival, keeping in focus the massive changes taking place in technology, the emergence of new markets, new knowledge in managing business and the creation of shareholder values. Equally important is that it should provide the space and opportunity to future generations to fulfil their chosen path. Wockhardt is just an option. They must be able to pursue a different path for which they should have financial accessibility.

Finally, we adopted the idea of a family charter, a family council and a succession plan. I felt I had already succeeded in ensuring gender balance and also in defining the individual roles of my three children. The charter and the council were needed for going forward, and also to institutionalize many of the good practices that we had already adopted.

I would be the chairman of the council and my three children its members. I involved all of them in the drafting of the charter and incorporated all their views. The family council meets once every three to four months. Nafisa is not a member of the council, nor are the spouses of my children. I preferred it that way to make the point that the council would focus only on business matters, so only those directly involved in the business would be its members. By keeping Nafisa out, I made that distinction between family and the family council. I also had a long-established rule that none of our family's in-laws, including the spouses of my children, would work for the company. This was meant to avoid any conflict of interest or any cross-connections in managing the business and at the same time maintain cordial family relations.

I wrote our charter in a manner that allows for some flexibility and provides individual members with the space for creative thinking. I did not want the charter to suffocate individual initiative or curb freedom of action. I kept this space because we are a research-based organization and creativity is the essence of research. No one should feel stifled in any way and adequate space should be available for initiative and risk-taking. Moreover, I want this charter to survive even the next generation. When I am gone, my children and grandchildren and subsequent generations should also feel that it is a fair system that has served their interests well and has given them the space for further growth and change.

*Habil Khorakiwala with his children and grandchildren.*
*From left: Son-in-law Ali Nabee, Samina (Huzaifa's wife), Umaima*
*(Murtaza's wife), wife Nafisa with Miqdad and Zayn, Muayyad, Habil Khorakiwala,*
*Zahabiya, Huzaifa, Murtaza with his son Ali*

Finally, we took care to ensure that all the provisions of the charter conformed to the law of the land. Once the draft was ready, I asked my children to vet it and give their inputs. I was delighted when I found them investing considerable time in studying all the provisions, discussing these with E&Y and Berjis, and coming up with their own suggestions to improve the draft. We incorporated all the suggestions made by them and the charter was adopted in 2014. I am satisfied that it will survive my passing away.

The only real legacy that I want to leave behind for my children is the fundamental values that our family has come to represent in doing business. I think I have instilled in them a deep respect for these values. As long as they adhere to these core values of fairness, transparency, commitment to learning and research and contributing to human well-being through the work we do, they are free to do anything else they like to take the company forward. I know situations change all the time; what is relevant today may not be relevant tomorrow in the world of business. But values remain. What one regards as good values today, should also be the good values of tomorrow.

*Zahabiya Khorakiwala with husband Ali Nabee and daughter Aaida*

*Murtaza Khorakiwala with wife Umaima and sons Ali and Zayn*

*Huzaifa Khorakiwala with wife Samina and sons Miqdad and Muayyad*

*Habil Khorakiwala with his entire family. Standing (from left): Zayn, Umaima, Murtaza,*
*Samina, Ali Nabee and Miqdad. Sitting (from left): Ali, Muayyad, Nafisa, Zahabiya wit[h]*
*on her lap, Habil Khorakiwala and Sugrabai Latif*

I had the good fortune of knowing Habil Khorakiwala for almost a decade and a half. My first encounter with him was based on very positive inputs I had received about him and his company from several top entrepreneurs. I was then Secretary-General of FICCI. I happened to be in Mumbai for an international event and decided that I would attempt to acquaint myself with a widely acclaimed entrepreneur—someone who apparently was continuously innovating at the cutting edge. So, I decided to drop by at Habil's office and get a feel of what innovations he was crafting and how those could become benchmarks for the rest of India's manufacturing sector in the decades ahead. We had not known each other before and, therefore, it was truly the first encounter.

Within the short span of our meeting, I realized that not only was Habil a professional himself, but was creating professionalized institutions that would soon compete with the best in the world. His humility and transparency touched me immediately. This first encounter slowly led to a multidimensional interaction over the next decade and a half. At the very first instance, I knew that it would be wonderful to have Habil to lead the apex chamber of India, FICCI, at some point in the near future.

I had the opportunity of observing him very closely and learning from Habil during his tenure as president of FICCI during the year 2006–07. We travelled together, across the world, for global conferences, business meetings, think-tank roundtables, scholarly seminars and engaged with prime ministers and presidents of many nations. I noticed that Habil had a special knack for fresh ideas and new perspectives, with the motivation to convert some of these ideas into reality in the world of commerce and industry. I noticed that he would often speak about the challenge of scaling up incubated ideas.

During our sojourn together, I recall an unforgettable day. We were in Bengaluru for a conference and Habil strongly suggested that on the way to the airport, I stop with him at his hospital and see for myself what he had been able to create. As we approached the hospital, I noticed that the insignia and seal of Harvard University were on the top of the building.

Having spent many years in the academic world of the US, I know that Harvard would not lend its insignia and seal without a great deal of due diligence and introspection. In fact, I had not seen the Harvard branding in any building in India. So I asked Habil as to how this near-impossible task was achieved. He explained how Harvard Medical School did a detailed audit of his hospital and came to the conclusion that it was worthy of a joint effort, where Harvard would be willing to lend its brand value to Habil's hospital. Needless to say that when we walked in and went through some of the most advanced technologies and resources, I could sense as to why Harvard Medical School would consider associating with Habil Khorakiwala's efforts. I still recall that on the top floor of the hospital, he had created a garden around which rooms occupied by international patients were located. One of the patients, sitting in the garden, had flown down from the US to get a hip replacement at a fraction of a cost and said to me that the quality of surgery and patient-care was comparable to the best in the world. I was proud to experience at first hand what India can provide in competition with the developed world.

It is noteworthy that Habil not only builds institutions and creates value, but he also knows when to unlock the value and move on to a new challenge. So, few years after my visit to his hospital, I came to learn that he had unlocked the value in his hospitals business, handing over many units to Fortis. This enabled him to not only move into other areas, but also improve the quality of the hospitals business that he retained.

Ever since I returned to Kolkata, in 2011, with a tectonic shift in my career from the corridors of power in New Delhi to the humble villages and burgeoning urban habitats of 93 million people of West Bengal, I have not had the occasion to interact with Habil. Today, as a member of the cabinet of the government led by Chief Minister Mamata Banerjee, I am privy to many policy changes and practices that she has introduced in the health sector, along with the construction of forty multispeciality hospitals at the subdivisional level in the state. Many of these hospitals have been built by Larsen & Toubro and Shapoorji Pallonji through transparent competitive bidding. The other day, when I saw one such hospital in a remote part of the state, I remembered the multispeciality hospital I had seen over a decade ago in Bengaluru and I recalled Habil's explanation of what was innovative in his hospital, which was striving for the best in healthcare in the world.

I am sure that since 2012, there has been yet more innovation in his pharmaceutical and biotechnology businesses, enriching the economy of our nation. I remain an admirer of Habil Khorakiwala's indomitable spirit to excel.

**Amit Mitra**, Finance Minister, West Bengal;
former Secretary-General, FICCI

## Chapter 10

# Managing Change

*Courage is what it takes to stand up and speak;*
*courage is also what it takes to sit down and listen.*

—Winston Churchill

*M*y professional life began in Mumbai and took me into the dry districts of Maharashtra. The first change I had to manage was this move. It was not easy, but I cherished every bit of the experience. By 1980, I was ready to take the next step. We could not remain a single-facility formulations manufacturer. I wanted to enter bulk drugs and then venture beyond India. I knew that we had the potential to go global, but I wanted to prepare myself before taking the next step. The logical thing to do would be to go back to the classroom and re-energize my thinking cells.

Wockhardt was still a small company, narrowly focused on manufacturing known formulations and physically located in a narrow geography in western India. My basic training in pharmacy at Purdue had run its course. It was time for me to widen my horizons and acquire new organizational understanding. I knew that we had to evolve into a multi-business company, with multiple locations for manufacturing, and grow on the basis of research and investment in biotechnology and the wider healthcare business.

The Advanced Management Programme was a thirteen-week course for CEOs. I discovered that at thirty-nine, I was the youngest member, of a class of 160. I was overcome by trepidation. I had arrived in Boston imagining I had seen quite a bit of life. I was overawed in my first interactions as I began to discover that others had lived equally, and more, adventurous lives as risk-takers and entrepreneurs. I did not let that sense of unease daunt me. After all, the very purpose of enrolling in such a programme and spending time in a place like Harvard was to judge one's own learning and experience against that of others who had also made their mark in business.

I summoned all my reserves of self-confidence and decided that I was at Harvard to learn and would return home better equipped to take on new challenges. The programme was designed to ensure that eight participants would live together for its duration. All of us came from different industry backgrounds, with different experiences and from different countries. My group had John Harris from the UK, David Lovette from Canada, Buz Buzzard from the US (although he had worked in Indonesia and other countries), George Petty from AT&T in the US and Terrence Renaud and John Vaughey also from the US but from different industries. Living together helped us in creating deep friendships and develop new learnings in various walks of life and business.

For all my initial nervousness, I took to the course like a fish to water. I got involved in every case study and every classroom discussion. With each class hour, I rediscovered myself. I began listing the areas where I felt I needed to learn more and areas where I felt I could in fact contribute to the learning process.

The programme had a mixed lot of business leaders from varied backgrounds. One CEO was running a water management company, another was a banker in Arkansas, yet another was into cement manufacturing. The diverse backgrounds of the attendees made every interaction meaningful.

I was in the pharma business, but my expertise was mainly in manufacturing and marketing. In these fields of business I was confident I knew more than what I was being taught. But the real learning came in the wider field of corporate strategy and business viability. The most important learning for me within the first week of the programme was that I found my very unconventional way of approaching problems and challenges was quite okay. My professors appreciated that and encouraged me to continue to do so.

Doing business is not just about organization, manufacturing and marketing. It is about imagination and judgement. There is a difference between being a businessman and being an entrepreneur. One can be good at doing business by doing the predictable, the expected, walking a path already defined. Management schools teach you how to be good at that. Enterprise is often a walk into the unknown. The Harvard programme boosted my self-confidence because I realized that it was all right to be unconventional.

More than the classroom discussions, it was the out-of-classroom interactions with faculty that proved to be most stimulating. We had a professor of finance, Sam Hays, the author of many books, who would make all kinds of assertions to provoke response. For example, when investing in stocks, he would say, most look at a company's financials—the balance sheet, income statement and so on. But one must look for something more—for 'hope'. Investment is about the future, not the past. All that data tells you is the story of the past. How do you judge a company's future? Do you find 'hope' in its financials? Entrepreneurship is about the future. What kind of hope can you create for your organization that the stock market can value and represent?

Then there was Professor Milt Brown. He was head of marketing. As I have said, I thought I was the cat's whiskers in marketing. He made me realize I needed to learn more and question many of my assumptions. A third professor who left a deep impression on me was

Professor Vance. He was an elderly, genial man with a fine grasp of public policy. Understanding public policy is vital to any businessman, especially in the pharma sector. He gave me a good insight for analysing policy.

Then there was a professor dealing with ethics and another who covered gender issues, which was already an issue for business leaders to think about. The breadth of all these topics made me realize the diversity of issues that one needs to look at when starting and running a business. The programme underscored the importance of the moral and ethical fabric that forms the backdrop to doing business in an open society. Sensitizing managers to these issues is important. I was struck by the fact that at least 10 per cent of all our case studies had to do with ethics in business.

Having spent twelve of the thirteen weeks doing their own thing and also participating in programmes arranged for them, our spouses joined us for the thirteenth week of the programme. Nafisa found that week's exposure interesting for two reasons. First, she found the lectures interesting and got a feel for what we had been up to for those three months. But, more importantly, she told me that the week's programme gave her a better understanding of what I had been doing all those years that I had been away from home, building Wockhardt. The last week's programme helped us bond even more.

One of the nice things about doing such a course is that one makes some very good friends for life. Nafisa and I grew close to a group of around seven couples. We decided to spend a few days together at Martha's Vineyard, the lovely island retreat near New York. It was still very cold in late April, so we would start the day with a concoction of beef broth and vodka. The lovely beaches of Martha's Vineyard were perfect for morning walks, with interesting conversations about how people from different parts of the world see life and society. The evenings were great fun. One night, we unknowingly entered a gay bar and exited as soon as we came to know about the place.

We returned home rejuvenated. I was charged with a renewed sense of pushing ahead. My first responsibility upon my return was to set up our first bulk drug unit. Over the next decade, our range of business widened as we entered new product lines and increased our capacity, setting up new facilities and tapping new sources of funds. In 1992, we went public; and in 1994, we raised funds globally issuing Global Depository Receipts (GDRs). As I have already mentioned, we were the first Indian pharma company to issue GDRs. In 1996, Wockhardt became the first Indian company to buy a British firm, Wallis Laboratories. I cannot explain the range of changes that we had to manage over a short decade.

∽

In business there are many dimensions to change. Just as the human body changes with time, so too do firms. Apart from such organic growth, firms must also explore opportunities arising out of inorganic growth, as activities expand and multiply. Growth brings with it many changes. There is an increase in organizational complexity. External competition acquires a whole new dimension as new markets and new players begin to focus on you and the growth of your firm. Then there is technological change, a largely autonomous variable, but for a research-based organization, some of that technological/technical change can come from managerial decisions. Growth also often entails a change in the company's geography of operation—both in terms of markets and manufacturing locations. Geographical change in turn could impact corporate culture. Finally, there is the external environment—ranging from the role of independent directors and the functioning of the board to regulatory issues, government policy on pricing and patents, and so on. Change management requires focus on all these fronts.

It should be immediately obvious that the macro aspects of managing change are as important, perhaps even more so, than the micro aspects of managing change. In other words, it is not just how we do what we do but also what is happening around us that defines our success. A good CEO hopes to have a firm grip on the former, but one must strive to acquire a grip on the latter as well. Therein lies the challenge of managing change.

## Geography and Language

When our operation was based only in Mumbai, our organization too was very simple. As the geography of our operations changed, the range of our activities widened and so did the complexity of our business. The move from Mumbai to Aurangabad immediately meant that we needed managerial capacity to deal with a new place and a new set of actors—local district officials, our own staff, and so on. A change in geography often also means changes in organizational culture and values. You need managers who can manage the new diversity. Mark my words—you need managers, not followers. People who can take decisions and implement them. My colleagues in Aurangabad could not wait to connect with me in Mumbai and then take a decision. Those were also difficult days for communication. We had no mobile telephony or videoconferencing. I had to depend on those who were located in our new manufacturing centres to take the right decision.

Manufacturing is a complex activity. It involves interaction between people, technology and organization. The first problems that come up as a firm grows are issues dealing with human relations. What goes by the name of 'industrial relations' is in fact nothing but human relations. Once you go outside India, you are dealing with a different reality in terms of people, policy, law and markets. Each time we have located our plants in a new place, I have visited the location repeatedly to be able to properly integrate the new team with the existing ones. It is only when I felt confident that I knew the new place, the new people and the new policy environment that I would leave the entire operation in the charge of a competent colleague. Once the initial ground is well laid, one does not have to worry.

An aspect of changing geography that is of great importance is language. Both in Gujarat and Maharashtra as well as in the US and the UK I had no problem relating to staff who were better equipped in their mother tongue. I could communicate directly with the staff in their language. I was able to appreciate the nuances of what they were saying. But in Germany and France, I did come up against the language barrier. I found that it was quite significant in both countries. I do believe that our US and UK operations were smoother than our European ones, mostly owing to the language barrier—both within the company and in relating to local authorities.

Culture

The problem of language is probably associated more with that of culture than geography, but culture is a much larger issue in management. This issue of culture comes up specially with inorganic growth, as I discovered when we acquired Merind. Each organization had its own culture. McKinsey helped me to resolve this issue. They advised that the Wockhardt management processes, systems and culture were good for a performing organization. They also advised that one should not expend too much effort in integrating all aspects of the organization. One should focus on value creation. Therefore, with Merind and other subsequent acquisitions, I explained the Wockhardt culture, processes and performance dimensions. I suggested that only one approach would work in the larger interest of the organization and, therefore, I requested all senior managers and leaders to adapt to the Wockhardt way of working. I am very happy that the majority of the organizations have accepted this reality and we have been able to create significant value out of most of our acquisitions.

## Competition

Competition, more than growth, is a key determinant of change. Growth can be planned and the change that comes with it managed. Competition can create unexpected situations enforcing change from the outside. Of course, there can be healthy and unhealthy competition. In an otherwise progressive business environment, one bad egg can turn healthy competition into an unhealthy one, adopting questionable practices. The fact is that healthy competition benefits all and unhealthy competition benefits no one. Yet both market environments exist and one must deal with both situations. In any case one cannot wish away competition. One can only outsmart it.

Often, potential competitors pretend to compete but end up having implicit market-sharing arrangements. The classic example is that of Kodak and Polaroid. As long as they served their individual markets they were not in direct competition with each other. But when Polaroid chose to enter Kodak's terrain, the latter hit back with a range of new products that wiped Polaroid out. Polaroid had underestimated its rival's potential for taking on competition. It had assumed that an implicit non-compete arrangement was a sign of the potential rival's weakness. It did not prepare for the contingency wherein that rival has inner reserves with which it can take on competition. It's a lesson we learn from the natural world, from animal life. It's called the survival instinct. One's ability to survive derives not just from one's visible strengths that are known to a potential rival, but equally, if not more, from one's invisible strengths that can be deployed in battle to vanquish the attacker.

In pharma, as in so many sectors now, technology provides disruption. It is the single biggest definer of the nature of competition. When we found ourselves in a competitive situation with Core Parenterals, I found they wanted a market-sharing agreement aimed at eliminating competition. I was clear in my mind that we were ready to take on competition. More importantly, I had to convince Core Parenterals that I was in fact ready to beat competition. That kind of confidence can itself unnerve your competitor. I had learnt some valuable lessons at Harvard about how one can deal with competition following an entirely different and innovative strategy.

## Complexity

I have always believed that if you do a simple thing in a simple way and produce a simple product, you face much higher competitive pressure. That is because others can easily imitate you. Where value creation is limited, the chance of facing new competitors in the market is higher. On the other hand, if your product is complex, the production methodology is complex, the technology is complex, the geography of your market and sourcing is complex, competition will find entry costs higher. Complexity reduces competition.

Each time we had to decide on a new product, a new technology, a new market, a new facility, my simple question to my colleagues would be—are we making the production and marketing process more complex or less? If we were increasing the level of complexity I would approve the decision. There may be elegance in simplicity, but complexity gives you better control on your own destiny.

Consider the example of hospital care. We started with tertiary care, which is a very complex management organization. We cut our teeth in this line of business setting up a heart institute in Bengaluru. On the other hand, we also set up a day care centre in Kolkata. The two were at the polar ends of the complexity–simplicity curve. Day care is not a speciality service. Entry costs are low, returns are low. It was an interesting thing to do only because it was innovative. We were pioneers in the day care business in Kolkata. We introduced lithotripsy in kidney stone management to Kolkata, as also laser technology for eye care.

The Kolkata project did well, but I found the Bengaluru project far more challenging. Heart care is a far more complex business. It is not all about technology, as kidney and eye care have become. There are, what I would call, soft areas of management in terms of clinical facilities, the kind of doctors one has, and so on that make a difference to the patient and, therefore, to the business. Over time we moved away from the 'simple' business of day care and focused on the 'complex' business of heart care. We then moved from single-speciality to multi-speciality hospitals.

Once you enter the business of complex organization management, simple organizations are not only unexciting but often, managing them is no longer that easy, because your thinking process and mindset have evolved. Going from simple to complex is often easier than going from complex to simple. The difference between the two is not just in terms of technology, medical skills, hardware costs and so on. The difference lies essentially in the soft skill of human management. Hospitals get their branding not from how big they are or how much new technology they have, or even how many doctors they have, but how well they are able to utilize and deploy their human skills, their technical skills, and secure patient confidence and satisfaction by providing superior medical outcomes. This is a very complex process indeed.

What is true for hospitals is even more true for pharmaceuticals. It is the complexity of the research, design, production and marketing process that gives one an edge over competition. The complexity of science and technology, of the thinking process of our researchers, bolsters our competitive strength. In an area like API, where simple technologies exist, I chose to opt for more complex ones, as in the case of metoprolol.

Complexity also implies we remain a learning organization. That is key to growth in a knowledge-based business like ours. One has to create a learning environment that constantly challenges the inquisitive mind and keeps our researchers and managers on their toes. Finance can be borrowed, technology can be bought, markets can be acquired. But knowledge-based manufacturing requires the creation of a learning environment that creates a greenhouse of growth based on internal intellectual resources.

## Technology

India's economic opening in 1991, the decision to join the WTO and adhere to its new rules pertaining to intellectual property rights and our own decision to acquire a global market footprint for our products completely changed the wider context within which we were operating. Not only were we now required to think global, but we also had to act global. The first step in that direction was to graduate from simpler levels of technology, scale and product mix to more complex levels. Globalization immediately underscored the importance of investing in research and technology. With this investment came the need to know how to manage the transition and the new growth process. It also meant hiring more skilled people and knowing how to manage the highly skilled

The induction of new technology is not a mechanical process. It is not simply about building new facilities and hiring new people. One has to integrate the old with the new. One has to manage the existing staff while learning how to deal with a new, more skilled set. Technological change has organizational implications. With new machines come new people, new practices, new problems, new opportunities, new markets, new suppliers, new managers and so much else. The technological upgrade of a product line is a complex managerial process.

*Habil Khorakiwala with good friend Adi Godrej, chairman of the Godrej Group,
at one of Wockhardt's award presentations for staff members*

For me, the biggest challenge was to get the right people. I was obsessed about whom we hired. Every individual matters. I would see some companies move faster than us in implementing their plans for modernization and widening their product range. I believed in the hare-and-tortoise metaphor. Better move slowly, but surely. In the end, taking the correct steps makes the journey more rewarding.

If one tries to do everything at the same time that may in fact adversely impact overall performance. After all, the performance of an organization is a collective effort. As the composition of that collective changes, the organization must know how to manage the new collective to get better results than before. Technology alone cannot ensure that.

As we moved from formulations to bulk drugs, we learnt how to manage the new technologies that came with change. This takes time and I realized that I must have the patience to allow time to play its role. This transition need not have taken the time it did because we had the required competence within the organization to facilitate that transition. Yet, it did take time. Perhaps our learning was slow. Perhaps our organization was not yet ready. Our entry into nutrition took even more time, even though competition at home was limited given that very few companies were in that line of business at the time. But I believed in the adage 'slow and steady wins the race'.

But the greatest challenge was the transition to biotechnology. Biotechnology is a complex process from a business perspective. There are many sub-technologies in biotechnology ranging from yeast to insulin. Erythropoietin is a complex protein and involves a very different technology. Large volume parenterals (LVPs) involve an entirely different organization from a technology point of view. In entering the biotechnology space we moved quickly across a large range of new technologies. That we were able to absorb them easily and quickly is a testimony to our organizational strength.

## People

Manufacturing, as an activity, involves people. Of course, in the modern robotics-based manufacturing systems the number of people involved has gone down dramatically. But in a research-based activity like ours, people are at the centre of the production process. We were fortunate to have even in the early years of our operation highly competent professionals working for us, like S.P. Singh. He developed the early dextropropoxyphene and dextromethorphan technology. He established our bulk drugs facility. In biotechnology, I was very fortunate to have met Maharaj Kishen Sahib and convince him to join us. In pharmaceuticals, there are many scientists who have contributed to technology development at various stages. In drug discovery, we had Noel D'Souza in the beginning, but the key leader has been Mahesh

Patel. Mahesh has made a real difference to Wockhardt and has helped establish our research programme, conceptualizing our approach and the processes. In stem cell research, where we are still in the very early stages of R&D, I was fortunate that Vijay Sharma agreed to lead the team. I would venture to say that we are perhaps the only company in India doing serious research in stem cell therapy.

On the management side, I have been fortunate to have great leaders who have always accepted challenges and given exceptional results. Each one of them has contributed in a significant manner to the growth of Wockhardt and helped manage the process of change. I have always considered my own role in the company as one of encouraging and inspiring others to perform to the best of their ability. Sometimes, I am criticized for my blind faith in our people, but faith and trust are key to human relationships. In the early years, I was myself completely involved in everything we did. Over time, I have learnt to delegate by trusting my colleagues.

It is important to remember that one can instruct and direct a manager dealing with manufacturing, finance, labour relations or marketing. But when it comes to research, one cannot direct one's colleagues. One has to learn to understand them and be able to guide them. The approach we have adopted is that they give me feedback on what they are doing and I understand. We have KOL meetings, which give me an opportunity to understand what they are doing and be able to guide them.

Our first KOL meeting, as I have mentioned earlier, was in Chicago and was for three full days. The general pattern followed for these meetings is that on the first day, our own scientists and invitees from prominent institutions in the field evaluate our work and share scientific data. My role is to observe and understand how they do what they do. On the second day, these experts offer suggestions to guide our researchers. On the third day, the dialogue and discussion becomes intense and focused. Once I see that the most brilliant minds in the fields we are working in are in agreement with what our researchers are doing, I give them my full support. They are then free to move on, work on their own, without interference and resource constraints. That is the only way research can be integrated into manufacturing.

Once we know what products we are likely to come out with, I then challenge my marketing team to find the market, identify competition and evaluate our own products vis-à-vis any existing competition. Our scientists then evaluate the available alternatives in the market against what they are developing to be sure that they are on to something new and different.

In the long term a company needs a shared vision, and it is my responsibility to devise one. To handle the rest we have enough good people. Once a year I send out a message to all my colleagues, updating them on my ideas about where we are headed. I have stayed away from micromanagement. But, I keep my door open to anyone who wishes to meet me for any reason. I make sure that they do not just come and refer a problem to me, but go away having thought of potential solutions. My job is to offer my view. It is up to them to accept it or not. Of course, I am very candid in offering my own assessment of what they say, but I have seen that most take it in the right spirit. Being nice all the time does not always work. It does not earn your colleagues' respect for you. Giving negative feedback is as important as giving positive feedback. If I do not tell them what is wrong, I am not giving them the true picture or an opportunity to correct mistakes. Management is, after all, a behavioural science. Indeed, it is more art than science.

Policy

Every business functions within a defined policy and regulatory space. The pharma business, more so. At every stage, from research to marketing, public policy impacts us. In India, more so. From patents to price control, from clinical trials to company law the policy that defines the scale and scope of our business is becoming only more complex. Much of this is understandable and necessary. After all, we are in the business of life.

For that very reason it is important for regulators to realize that science is an evolving discipline and regulation must be knowledge based. When science changes, regulations and rules governing such science based manufacturing must catch up. The USFDA is the largest regulatory body in the world. They are sensitive to new science and try to adapt regulation to new knowledge. The Europeans are even more knowledge based in their regulation. One can explain in scientific terms what one is doing and the regulator immediately understands. There is one difference between the US and European systems. The US officials may understand the science behind a procedure, but they stick to the word of the rulebook. They are system-bound. European regulators are prepared to accept a purely scientific interpretation whereas the US regulators will not accept any interpretation if their system is not followed. Whatever one has given in one's ANDA must be followed in letter and spirit completely. European regulators are normally postgraduates and PhDs in a relevant discipline. They have empathy for research and researchers. The USFDA people are rarely science graduates.

India had a proud record of hiring talented regulators who understood the science. In the past, one could meet a drug controller and explain what one was doing in scientific terms. Unfortunately, however, over time our regulatory institutions have been taken over by administrators, often of the Indian Administrative Service (IAS), with little or no knowledge of the science involved. So, while the US system is rule-bound and the European approval process is based on scientific principles, the Indian approval process has become increasingly bureaucratic and arbitrary.

On top of such regulatory constraint comes an increasingly complex company law. The first Manmohan Singh government set up the J.J. Irani Committee on Company Law in December 2004 with a view to: (a) bringing about compactness by reducing the size of the Act and removing redundant provisions; (b) enabling easy and unambiguous interpretation of the law by recasting the provisions of the law; (c) providing greater flexibility in rule-making to enable timely response to the ever-evolving business models; and (d) protecting the interests of the stakeholders and investors, including small investors. This policy intervention was aimed at making life easier for business. In practice, I would argue, it has had the opposite effect. The Indian bureaucracy has succeeded in making it even more difficult to do business in India, especially in a research-based sector like ours.

The new law has made the functioning of a company board highly procedure oriented, without in any significant way improving corporate governance. There is now an obsession with routine and procedural compliance. So many forms to be filled, so many markers to be ticked off, so many records to be kept. Has all this improved the ease of doing business and the quality of corporate governance? I am not sure. What it has certainly done is to increase the time spent on routine compliance and managerial costs. One good consequence of all this has been to increase computerization of records, improving the access to a range of internally generated data. That has certainly improved internal audit systems.

One of the objectives of the new company law was to improve corporate governance at the top. It is a moot question whether this objective has been achieved given the spate of high-profile controversies around the issue of board accountability and corporate governance. The real strength of a company board lies in the quality of its membership. At Wockhardt, I have been fortunate in having been able to attract a large number of highly qualified, respected, talented and independent-minded individuals to join our board over the years.

The new company law gives the impression that independent

board members must represent minority shareholder interests. Even the Securities and Exchange Board of India (SEBI) rules have a bias in favour of minority shareholders as if they are vulnerable to the predatory tactics of majority shareholders. If that is the suggestion, I disagree. All board members, including promoter representatives, must at all times uphold the best interests of the company as a whole, and therefore of all shareholders. The one thing that independent members of the board should ensure is that the promoter does not siphon away money from the company to the detriment of the minority shareholders and the company as a whole. Maintaining an eagle-eye on related party transactions is important.

*Wockhardt board members. From left: Huzaifa Khorakiwala, Baldev Arora, V.K. Jairath, Habil Khorakiwala, Murtaza Khorakiwala, Tasneem Mehta, Aman Mehta, Shekhar Datta, D.S. Brar and Sanjaya Baru*

When a board is overseeing the functioning of a stand-alone company in a single line of business, it is easier to monitor what is happening.

But when the board has to oversee the functioning of a multi-company conglomerate and analyse consolidated data, compliance issues become more complex. In such a case, while the promoter may have only the group interest in mind, board members must take care of the individual interests of all entities within the conglomerate. Here, I must add, the new company law has made a positive contribution.

We went public in 1992. Overall, our experience has been positive. I am very candid with my board members, even in difficult times. I respect all my board members and whenever they express a view different from mine, I try my best to accommodate their views. If they want any additional information even on any unpleasant issues, I do not hide it from them. This has enabled us to function well together.

A disturbing trend in India in recent years is that we tend to imitate global bad practices while ignoring global best practices. We borrow all the wrong ideas from Europe and the US when it comes to corporate governance, without borrowing the larger policy regime they have had for years, which has enabled their companies to go global. I find most East Asian countries have stayed away from such imitative behaviour, focusing instead on making their companies globally competitive. We have put in place systems that can be handled easily if the courts are efficient in dealing with issues of compliance. However, our judicial process is cumbersome and costly. All that excessive regulation has done is enrich the legal fraternity of corporate lawyers and arbitrators.

In the end, from a national standpoint, what the country needs is a policy framework for corporate growth and for ease of doing business and a strategy that promotes competition and the competitive advantage of Indian firms. The rules that govern the entry and exit of firms must be made far simpler, trusting investors rather than viewing them with suspicion.

Finally, price control. It has proved to be utterly ineffective over the years. In a competitive market, competition is the best form of price control. All that the government has to prevent is cartelization and price fixing. Let competition determine the price point. In the case of products with a limted number of producers, say, just three or four, the government can impose some rules to prevent price fixing. The generics business in India is highly competitive. There is no need for price control in generics. The model we have adopted is absurd. It destroys the market forces of competition. Companies with better quality systems, and that are compliant with US and European standards get better prices from doctors. The price control takes the average price of all similar drugs. This has an impact on quality culture.

Drugs under price control go out of the market within ten years. Companies promote products that are outside price control and reduce activities significantly for products that are under price control. Even if the drug is good for use, it is not available. Sometimes the government fixes a drug price below the manufacturing cost, making it unviable for the company to manufacture it. One thing that price control at home has done is force Indian companies to export to markets where there is no such control, or the margins available are higher. After all, as a research-based drug manufacturer, I need the financial resources to invest in our own growth. Price control has had a debilitating impact on growth.

Over the years, I have learnt a lot about people, places, science and technology by merely guiding my colleagues and creating a knowledge-based Indian company. In the end, we are a small company, but our learnings have been huge. That is why, in an era when knowledge is power, our science-based business has created a global Indian firm, firmly rooted in Indian soil.

Chapter 11

# Beyond Business

*Balance is not something you find, it's something you create.*

—Jana Kingsford

*I* was brought up in a business family that always emphasized the importance of striking a balance between work, family and society. In some ways, a joint family setting imposes that culture and value system on one. No one can be a recluse within a joint family. However busy one may be with work or studies, there are times when the family draws one out. In a city like Mumbai and in a community like ours, the neighbourhood too draws one out. But I would not be telling the truth if I did not confess that in the early years of my business, Nafisa took much of the responsibility for family and other social obligations.

If I did get drawn into larger social engagements, it was more often because of my father who had a very public profile. He was the Sheriff of Mumbai during a particularly difficult period in the city's recent history. Following a series of communal clashes and violence in 1993, resulting in many deaths, my father mobilized the general public to restore peace and communal harmony. He organized the longest human chain ever to be formed in Mumbai. It stretch for a hundred kilometres, linking over 150,000 citizens who stood quietly in solidarity holding hands. It had an electrifying effect on the city. My father, Alyque Padamsee, Julius Rebeiro and several other distinguished citizens also formed mohalla committees to restore communal harmony. It was an activity that we were all involved in.

*Habil Khorakiwala greets former Deputy Prime Minister of India, L.K. Advani, at a FICCI event*

As a young businessman, I was more interested in associating myself with business associations like the Rotary Club, the association of young Rotarians, and the Junior Jaycees, another such association of the young under the umbrella of Junior Chambers. Both were associations of young people with an interest in business, social work, and debate and discussion. At the Jaycees, I was chosen to be the editor of *Challenge*— the Jaycees journal—an experience I thoroughly enjoyed.

*Habil Khorakiwala with former Chief Minister of Jammu and Kashmir Farooq*
*Abdullah at Wockhardt Towers at a Ramzan Iftar.*
*Also seen are Habil Khorakiwala's father and wife*

In 1972, I served a term as president of the Malabar Hill Jaycees and the experience prompted me to run for the post of vice-president of the India branch of Jaycees International in 1974. It was my first exposure to politics and campaigning. I had to travel around India and address gatherings of Jaycees members in other cities. These groups were termed as 'caucuses'—a term borrowed from the political system in the United States. That was the only time I did any active political campaigning, seeking votes. While I ran for the post of vice-president, my friend the Late Murli Deora ran for the post of executive vice-president. He was certainly better prepared for the campaign than I was because he had badges with his photo printed on them, which he gave out to all Jaycees members around India during our campaign tours. But that did not help him win the election! Deora went on to become a successful parliamentarian, getting elected to the Lok Sabha from Mumbai.

In the 1980s, I became active with Rotary International and became president of the Rotary Club of Bombay North. These associations enabled a young business person like me to establish contacts with other like-minded persons and also widen my social circle. Doing business in a rapidly changing India, for even a small business firm like ours, was no longer just about sitting in office and dealing with other business partners. One needed to circulate socially, learn from others and build new relationships that were not only personally rewarding and socially interesting but were also profitable and relevant to one's line of business. I have retained my association with the Rotary Club over the years, participating actively in their programmes in India and abroad.

One activity of Rotary International that Nafisa and I became passionately involved in was the campaign for the universal eradication of polio. Rotary clubs around the world played an important role in the Global Polio Eradication Initiative that was launched in 1988 as a public–private partnership with the World Health Organization, UNICEF, the Bill and Melinda Gates Foundation and governments around the world working together. The Indian branch of Rotary International played an active role in this campaign. In 2011, India was declared polio-free. Today, only Afghanistan, Pakistan and Nigeria continue to report polio cases. The disease has been eradicated from the rest of the world. Nafisa and I participated actively in the campaign and contributed both with our time and money and we feel truly happy that we were able to contribute to this national achievement in our own small way. Given my long association with the Rotary Club I was proud to join its top-tier international membership, called the Arch C. Klumph Society. My friends and fellow members of the Rotary Club of Bombay North honoured me with the Club's highest status, 'Illustrious Member'.

One thing common to most of the first-generation entrepreneurs of the Indian pharmaceutical industry was our active involvement with public policy through two of our industry associations, the IDMA and the Indian Pharmaceuticals Alliance (IPA). The IDMA, created in 1961, has emerged as the most influential voice of the Indian pharma industry. The IPA is a body representing research-based Indian pharmaceutical companies. I was elected president of both organizations.

There was universal recognition within the industry of the fact that the growth of Indian pharma companies was almost entirely on account of the support they received from the Indian Patents Act of 1970. This was one of Prime Minister Indira Gandhi's most far-sighted policy interventions. In 1970, few in India, and fewer still around the world, imagined that India would one day have a globally competitive, research-based pharmaceutical industry. The fact that we have a domestic pharmaceutical industry today, and one that can stand proudly to claim global competence, is because of the twenty to twenty-five-year window of protection that the 1970 Patents Act gave us. In the early 1970s, 80 per cent of the drugs sold in India were manufactured by multinational corporations. Today, their share is down to below 15 per cent.

Many of us in the industry, like Yusuf Hamied, Parvinder Singh, Anji Reddy and so on played an active role in the IDMA. By the end of the 1980s, we realized that changes to the Patents Act were imminent. There was considerable pressure on India to modify and dilute the 1970 Act and to bring product patents under its coverage. If this had been done in a hurry, many Indian companies would have been hurt.

One section of the industry campaigned against any change in the law. Many of us associated ourselves with the sentiment and found support among several policymakers, including a senior judge of the Supreme Court, Justice V.R. Krishna Iyer. However, some of us, especially Parvinder, Anji and myself, recognized that some change was inevitable. Prime Minister Narasimha Rao had inaugurated the era of economic liberalization and decided that India would be a founding member of the WTO. The WTO was discussing Trade-Related Intellectual Property rights (TRIPs).

I found that not many in New Delhi were aware of the issues involved. Both our parliamentarians and many of the officials in the commerce ministry had to be tutored for them to be able to understand the issues. The IDMA took it upon itself to do so. I worked closely with a retired senior official of the Indian patents office, S. Vedaraman, to educate policymakers in Delhi. Apart from Justice Krishna Iyer and Vedaraman, several public-spirited personalities helped the industry at the time.

During my year of presidentship, the IDMA produced a 'Vision 2000' document for the pharmaceutical industry and I participated actively in its drafting. It gives me great satisfaction to say that the industry has indeed fulfilled that vision. We have achieved what we had set out to accomplish. One lesson I learnt from that entire experience was that government policy can be directed if we, in industry, are willing to take a holistic view and present that to policymakers. The politician and the bureaucrat resent self-serving petitions from business. But when business suggests something that would of course benefit it, but is also in the wider national and social interest, policymakers are willing to listen and learn. I find that most often their initial attitudes are shaped by ignorance and the arrogance of power. But if they recognize the merit of your argument, and if it serves their objectives too, then one can work with government to shape policy.

At least one reason why many of us in the pharma sector in the late 1980s and early 1990s may have come across as sincere and well meaning to Delhi's policymakers was the fact that we were all first-generation entrepreneurs, technically qualified and seeking to build a knowledge-based industry. Parvinder and I came from a business background, while Anji Reddy and Yusuf Hamied were technocrats. But all four of us were professionals with domain knowledge and we were seeking to place India on the global map.

Even as Indian companies were making their presence felt in the IT sector, the Indian pharma sector was also doing so. All this was happening in the 1990s, triggered by Prime Minister Rao's new policies. The IT companies were helped by the Y2K problem and the demand that created for Indian professionals. We had no such momentous opportunity, but by the turn of the century we too were making our mark globally. Like IT companies, we too entered the US market and the world took note.

∽

My exposure to public policy and to the corridors of power in New Delhi came in handy when FICCI invited me to become its president. My initial reaction to the invitation from FICCI, which came from a senior member and a past president, Kanti Kumar Poddar, was in fact negative. I was busy at Wockhardt and was not sure if I could devote much time to the many protocol-linked obligations as FICCI president. Realizing that I was not keen, Poddar went to my father and urged him to get me to reconsider. What finally changed my mind was a conversation with FICCI's dynamic secretary-general, Amit Mitra, who had played an important role in revitalizing FICCI. He urged me to accept the gesture made by the senior FICCI leader. Amit had something else in mind. FICCI had come to be known as an association of Marwari businessmen, while FICCI's new rival, the Confederation of Indian Industry (CII), had succeeded in projecting itself as an association of new enterprise. Not only was I not a Marwari, but I was also a first-generation entrepreneur in a dynamic new sector of Indian industry. Amit felt my presidency would enable him to project

FICCI in a different light to the media and the government of the day. Amit is a persuasive man and I got persuaded.

*Habil Khorakiwala with Pranab Mukherjee,*
*the then External Affairs Minister, and former President of India.*
*Alongside them is Amit Mitra, the then Secretary General of*
*FICCI and the current Finance Minister of West Bengal*

The FICCI presidency gave me exposure to policymaking at a very different level. As president of the IDMA and IPA, I had interacted mainly with sectoral ministries. As FICCI president, I got the opportunity to interact with senior national leaders from India and around the world. I had very stimulating discussions with Prime Minister Manmohan Singh and enjoyed the opportunity to interact with President Vladimir Putin of Russia, Chancellor Angela Merkel of Germany and Prime Minister Shinzo Abe of Japan, among others.

*Habil Khorakiwala welcoming German Chancellor Angela Merkel at a
joint meeting of FICCI and CII during her visit to India*

*Habil Khorakiwala welcoming Prime Minister of Japan, Shinzo Abe, during a FICCI
event. Also seen are Union Minister Suresh Prabhu, and
Finance Minister of West Bengal, Amit Mitra*

*Habil Khorakiwala welcoming Russian President Vladimir Putin*

Another highly competent member of Prime Minister Singh's ministry was Finance Minister P. Chidambaram. He rarely suffered fools. It was difficult to have a conversation with him if he was not convinced that he would learn something from talking to you. I had to call on him to convey FICCI's disapproval of the fringe benefits tax that he had imposed. It was a tax on various non-salary compensations provided to employees but included travel expenses. The pharmaceutical industry was particularly hurt because travel is an essential part of the work of marketing representatives. I went to meet the finance minister with trepidation but was pleasantly surprised to find him very receptive. He seemed to have realized that he had fallen prey to ill-thought advice from his tax officials. While the fringe benefits tax was not withdrawn by him, he did reduce the rate of taxation.

*Habil Khorakiwala with Kamal Nath,*
*former Union Minister of Commerce and Industry*

Both Kamal Nath and Chidambaram were incredibly knowledgeable people. As indeed was a minister in the Atal Bihari Vajpayee government with whom I had opportunities to interact, namely, Suresh Prabhu. It was also a pleasure to discuss policy with Prabhu. There are many ministers who are equally good, but regrettably not many are equally knowledgeable and approachable. By and large my experience has been that quite a few ministers and senior officials have little interest in what they are doing and even less interest in listening to one's views on specific issues. The normal practice is to ask you to send a note, or meet a junior official who is more familiar with the issues. Very rarely is there any serious follow-up or a serious dialogue to understand the issues and realities.

Even as my term at FICCI came to an end, I was quite excited when I received an invitation to participate in the World Economic Forum (WEF) at Davos in January 2008. The Davos meeting is an annual gathering of the world's most influential movers and shakers and I had heard so much about it that I was delighted to accept their invitation. Davos, a ski resort that is completely covered in snow in late January when the WEF meets, is a three-hour drive from Zurich airport. Every year thousands of people who run the world, the top businessmen, bankers, politicians, heads of governments, government officials, Nobel laureates, academics, scientists, artists, activists, and spiritual leaders, among others, congregate at this rather crowded place.

Driving from Zurich to Davos I viewed with awe the wide expanse of snow-clad mountains and plains. I had never seen such a spectacle even though I had travelled around Switzerland many times. What struck me at Davos was how particular they were about the environment. So much so that the car one travels by from Zurich must have a green certificate. They practised what they preached about the environment.

Given the large number of global VIPs and VVIPs gathering in that small town, the WEF takes full control of accommodation. The participants are given a few choices of hotels much in advance and the booking is done through the WEF. Some participants come early and enjoy skiing. The WEF has a permanent convention centre at Davos, which has several big and small conference halls. Typically, there are about two thousand participants in this annual event. The participation is by invitation only. Obviously, there is a hefty fee to be paid for the participating member and also for the guest.

The entire programme for the conference is available well before the date and most of the participants do advance booking for the programmes of their choice. Typically, there are thirty to forty sessions that take place simultaneously at various conference centres—some are workshops and some are very large conferences. The purpose of the WEF is primarily to understand the concerns and challenges of business leaders, politicians, economists and other stakeholders. At the meeting I attended, twenty-five to thirty prime ministers of various countries participated. The only exception, as I discovered, was that no US president has ever visited the Davos WEF.

Speakers included leaders from such diverse fields as medicine, art and culture, science, behavioural science, women's studies and environment. Given my varied interests, I chose to attend sessions on business, economics, medicine, behavioural science, art and culture, and social causes. Davos is, above all, about networking and conversations with leaders in business and all walks of life. Rarely does one have the opportunity to meet such a diverse lot in such limited space and time.

The networking opportunities at Davos range from small lunches, dinners and nightcaps at various restaurants to larger cocktail gatherings. One ends up with eight to ten invitations every day. I tried to attend as many as I could, also making sure that I attended the Harvard alumni gathering.

*Habil Khorakiwala, who was then FICCI president,*
*with actor Rekha (centre) and producer-director Yash Chopra (second from right) at*
*FICCI Living Legend in Entertainment Award Nite in 2007*

ൟ

I have always believed that the main reason why most East and Southeast Asian nations marched ahead of India in the post-colonial era was their investment in education. Japan, Korea, Taiwan, Singapore, Hong Kong and even China industrialized rapidly because they had laid the educational foundation for modernization. No industrial country in history has had less than 80 per cent literacy. But, literacy apart, the more important thing was the investment these countries made in technical education. In India, we have created centres of excellence at the top of the knowledge pyramid and our graduates coming from these institutions have been world class. The growth of knowledge-based industries like IT and pharma has been on account of the talent we have created. However, we have not paid as much attention to the rest of the knowledge pyramid, and certainly not to the creation of skilled workers. In a recent survey of the top 200 companies in India, it was found that together, all these companies found only 14 per cent of students coming from Indian universities to be adequately trained to take on a job without in-house training. Most companies have to invest in retraining and educating the people they hire. This shows the gap between demand and supply at critical levels in the knowledge pyramid. Universities have become out of touch with the educational needs of the economy as a whole. Political interference, commercialization and patronage-mongering in education have damaged our educational system. What purpose does a ministry of education serve if it cannot change the extant situation? We need professionally qualified regulators who can maintain standards, not ministers and bureaucrats who view institutions as their fiefdoms.

During my tenure as FICCI president, I had the opportunity to discuss this issue with Prime Minister Manmohan Singh, who agreed with me that India had neglected education and spoke at length about his own efforts to provide more funding for education. I got my first opportunity to make a difference to an educational institution when I was invited to become the chancellor of Jamia Hamdard, a deemed university located in Delhi. Jamia Hamdard has a long history, going back to the early years of the last century, but it was in 1972 that the late Hakeem Abdul Hameed, a renowned physician and a philanthropist, set up the Hamdard College of Pharmacy. As a student of pharmacy I felt honoured when invited to be the institution's chancellor. I devoted considerable time to strengthening the academic base of the institution.

*Habil Khorakiwala, during a discussion about the Indian economy, with former Prime Minister Manmohan Singh*

In 2016, I had to select a new vice-chancellor for the university and was keen that the person should be a scientist. I wanted to strengthen Jamia's science and technology departments. I was fortunate that a distinguished biologist, Professor Ehtesham Hasnain, was willing to join us. Hasnain had an impressive résumé, and had won several awards and honours in India and around the world. He was a Fellow of the American Academy of Microbiology and had, more recently, been vice-chancellor of the Central University of Hyderabad. I was delighted to find that Hasnain shared my passion for science. He also agreed with me that the university should introduce courses that would enable its students to find employment. One such course we introduced was in tourism. Travelling around the world to historic sites I would always be struck by the very knowledgeable tourist guides one encounters. In India we have very few trained guides. I felt a good course on tourism with a view to producing guides trained in history and archaeology would be a good idea. Both of us shared a commitment to excellence in education as well as to promoting socially relevant education.

∽

Of all the things I have done beyond business, nothing has given me more satisfaction than the work of the Wockhardt Foundation. Long before CSR became a buzzword in business circles, we set up the Foundation. Formed in September 2008, the Foundation has acquired global recognition for its excellent work in poverty alleviation and rural development. In the beginning, our company funded the Foundation fully, but now it is able to generate its own funding for an expanding range of activities. The one person who made all this possible is my son Huzaifa. Given his academic background, with an MBA from Yale, Huzaifa has been able to professionalize the Foundation's functioning and its programmes. In the beginning, I would act as a mentor to Huzaifa, but very soon I realized that he was way ahead of me in thinking and in his ability to execute a wide range of programmes. Moreover, once the children had grown up and Nafisa was no longer preoccupied with their education, she became actively interested in the world of the Foundation.

The Foundation functions on the basis of modern business practices. It has over three hundred staff who work hard, keep administrative costs low and ensure delivery of high quality services. Huzaifa tells me that his two watchwords are cost and quality. He is passionately committed to his programmes and is always brimming with new ideas. The Foundation's flagship programme is called 'Mobile 1,000'. It aims at operating a thousand mobile health vans in rural India, administering free primary healthcare to 25 million Indians every year. As of date, in early 2017, the Foundation had ninety-one Mobile 1,000 vans operating in eighteen states administering free primary healthcare to more than 2 million Indians in rural and remote parts of India.

*Habil Khorakiwala welcoming Chief Minister of Rajasthan Vasundhara Raje*

The sanitation programme—Pronto Toilets—is part of the prime minister's Swachh Bharat Abhiyan. Pronto Toilets has undertaken an ambitious plan of constructing more than 60,000 household toilets in Odisha. Other initiatives include health centres, Little Hearts, Pronto Bio Toilet, e-learning, Khel Khel Mein, the Wockhardt Skills Development Institute, SHUDHU water purification tablets, the Swachh the Bharat recycle machine and the Adarsh Gram Yojana.

I have always found it gratifying that members of the Wockhardt board take great interest in the work of the Foundation. Everyone sees it as being more than an important aspect of our corporate personality. It is a manifestation of our values and our commitment to social development. Mahatma Gandhi was right when he said that business leaders must view themselves as trustees of national wealth. To put it in Gandhiji's own words: 'Supposing I have come by a fair amount of wealth—either by way of legacy, or by means of trade and industry—I must know that all that wealth does not belong to me; what belongs to me is the right to an honourable livelihood, no better than that enjoyed by millions of others. The rest of my wealth belongs to the community and must be used for the welfare of the community.'

It is with that philosophy in mind that we have sought to live our life beyond business.

❧

## Chapter 12

# Going Forward

*Courage is grace under pressure.*

—Ernest Hemingway

$\mathcal{W}$ hen we entered into 2017, we were also entering our fiftieth anniversary year. I decided to send out a very special New Year's message to all my colleagues. Many of them have been with the company for a very long time. They have experienced the fact that every fifteen to twenty years, our company has been able to transform itself and reach new heights of performance. In the last twenty years, we have transformed ourselves from being a purely domestic Indian company to becoming a global organization. We have also become a public limited company. We have invested in R&D. We have acquired companies, which has helped us transform ourselves even as we transformed the companies we acquired.

I believe we are in the next major phase of transforming ourselves from a globalized manufacturing organization to a globalized research-based manufacturing organization. It will take a decade or more, but the direction is set. Our drug discovery team has focused for the last twenty years on antibiotic research and we have a significant portfolio of products that have a global reach. Almost all these products address the superbug menace the world is facing and provide life-saving solutions.

I told my colleagues that we are creating an organization capable of meeting our future aspirations. This means that we have to constantly look inwards as well as outwards, creating appropriate capabilities and competencies to deal with new opportunities and challenges. It is said that a snake sheds its skin every few years so as to get a new skin. Every growing firm in a competitive global market has to learn to do that.

My colleagues are aware of how we have faced challenges in the past, be they financial or technical. We have had issues with the regulatory compliance norms insisted upon by the USFDA. We had similar issues in the UK and we overcame those. I am confident that the USFDA chapter too will be behind us sooner rather than later. Our strength remains in our research capability, our manufacturing excellence and our complete transparency on both fronts. We have reset our priorities for our pharma research organization where the combined business opportunity of products approved, products filed and the products to be filed in the next three years will amount to $1 billion over the next five years. This, of course, is subject to an early resolution of USFDA remedial measures, which we are sure we will achieve.

We are also investing significantly in Phase II and Phase III clinical trials for our NCE programme for India and the global market. We should see WCK 771 and WCK 2349 in the Indian market hopefully by the latter half of 2019. As I have mentioned earlier, we will be in the US market for WCK 5222 and WCK 4282 in 2020 or early 2021, and a year later in various other markets in the world. We have a significant focus on biosimilars and our aim is to focus on emerging markets. We have also developed bio-betters, which we will introduce in India first and then take to the world market. We have full patent coverage for our bio-betters.

Our ambitions are built on our track record. As we enter our fiftieth year, I say with a sense of pride that we have not only built a research-based organization of global standards, but that we have also been able to produce affordable medicine, for which there is now a demand even in developed economies. It is this combination of achievements—the creation of a knowledge-based business and the manufacture of affordable medicines—that must motivate every Wockhardtian to contribute their best.

I have now devoted myself to building the Wockhardt of tomorrow—one that will retain its existing strengths and DNA, but evolve in as yet unimagined ways. I also believe that public policy is where I can contribute to nation building and Prime Minister Narendra Modi's dream of a New India. For example, in the field of healthcare, antibiotic resistance is increasing rapidly. Millions of people die every year due to it. There is a crying need to evolve and follow responsible and scientific methods in the use of antibiotics by doctors, have proper controls on distribution and ensure that pharmacies dispense antibiotics only on prescription. Even the government has to play a significant role in this. It may surprise you that many antibiotic combinations that are in use in India have no proper scientific basis through controlled clinical trials. Many of these antibiotic combinations have been tested in our laboratories and we have found that they do not increase the effectiveness of an antibiotic but, rather, increase the resistance of superbugs. The value of these combination antibiotics is ₹5,000 crore—nearly 25 per cent of all antibiotics prescribed in India. Even more, these combinations are not available anywhere else in the world. The continuous use of combinations that have not been properly clinically tested is the single greatest reason for superbug proliferation. I intend to take up the initiative to increase the responsible and scientific use of antibiotics—this will be called 'India's Antibiotic Stewardship' initiative.

⁂

As I reflect back on the Wockhardt odyssey, I realize that we have initiated many actions, some consciously and some subconsciously. This saga, this odyssey, has thrown up several lessons that entrepreneurs, managers and students of management may find interesting and of some value.

First, to ensure continued and sustainable growth, leaders and organizations must continuously look to the future, look around and look within. Imagining the future helps put into perspective unfolding phenomena and enables one to identify likely challenges and opportunities. Vision must be combined with clarity of purpose. To protect and ring-fence the business, the leader needs to have an antenna that can spot emerging competitors and their likely actions so as to ensure that the company runs faster than the competitors. This is possible only when an organization develops the internal capability to neutralize the threats and actualize the opportunities. Therefore, continued SWOT (strengths, weaknesses, opportunities and threats) analysis and looking into the mirror are sine qua non and these actions will help the leader to create tomorrow today, and take the organization ahead of its competitors.

Second, every business today faces a confluence of complexities, uncertainties, volatility and ambiguities. One will have to be like the ancient seafarers of the great oceans who navigated without a map and still managed to reach their destination by using the North Star as their guide. Leaders need a path-breaker spirit, courage and risk appetite to be able to create something different and new. Passion for one's area of expertise (in my case passion for science) will add manyfold to this quest for creating a path-breaking organization.

Third, leaders need the ability to constantly observe changes at the fringes, anticipate developments and connect apparently unrelated phenomena, in order to prepare the organization for the changes looming on the horizon. Leaders need to also connect the dots and read the patterns of opportunities, strengths and capabilities scattered within the organization in order to leverage the available strengths and capabilities.

Fourth, the continuous growth and sustainability of organizations depend on the core mantra of keeping the customer at the centre. In fact, organizations exist because of the customer. Leaders who have the compassion to understand not only the manifest needs but also the latent needs of the masses are the ones who are likely to meet customer needs. They continuously co-create products to meet customer needs and mitigate customer problems and in the process ensure the sustainability of their organizations.

Fifth, an entrepreneur must have an insatiable appetite for learning. A leader has to be a perpetual student, ceaselessly learning, meditating and reflecting on his experiences and translating this to the benefit of the organization. Leaders, and organizations, who stop learning slide rapidly downhill. The key to shifting an organization to the next orbit lies in the leader's ability to learn from the changing environment, as well as anticipate the future and use the power of imagination to think differently. It is through the power of learning combined with imagination that creative solutions are made possible.

Sixth, a business leader must learn the art of flying at 36,000 feet while, at the same time, hovering two inches above the ground. Some birds can do that—soar up to view the terrain, swoop down to pick a morsel. One must have a good understanding of both the big picture and the ground reality. Leaders who focus only on the grand vision may not be able to convert their visions into reality. On the other hand, those who focus only on the nitty-gritty will suffer from a myopic vision and actions. Both a vision and a grip on ground realities are required for the successful conversion of ideas into action.

Seventh, great organizations are built around people on the foundations of trust, commitment, empowerment and a Himalayan purpose—a cause that mobilizes the collective energy and inspires people to give beyond their best. In today's era most pillars of competitive advantage can be imitated and improved, barring people power. This can never be cloned and is the key source of the competitive edge for an organization. To harness people power to the fullest, leaders must delegate and rally people around a larger cause not through a diktat but through positive influence. Above all, they must put the right person in the right job.

Eighth, a long-distance runner in business must remain ethical and transparent. There are no shortcuts. A leader must have a clear list of 'Dos and Don'ts' that the entire organization understands. One must have short- and long-term goals, and strike a balance between profit-making and wealth creation. Leaders should have wealth-creating zeal and passion so that organizations are built on unshakeable foundations. Leaders must ensure that the interests of all stakeholders are met. They must try to integrate and align the interest of the organization with the interest of the stakeholders.

Finally, a business leader's professional journey, of building a great and enduring organization, runs parallel to her personal journey, of emotional and intellectual development. By virtue of their position in the organization, leaders tend to be viewed as role models and people tend to imitate and follow their behaviour and actions. In fact leaders live in fragile glass houses—especially in today's world of the democratization of information through social media. Reputations built over a lifetime can be ripped apart in no time. The leader is constantly in the glare of the public eye and therein lies the challenge of remaining balanced, calm and focused, matching practice with what is preached.

My daughter Zahabiya put it well in a recent interview to *The Economic Times*. She said the one important lesson she had learnt from me was what she called 'the power of calm—how to maintain grace under pressure, learn from challenges and take the ups and downs of life in one's stride. His Holiness the Dalai Lama put it very nicely when he said, 'A calm mind is good for our physical health, but it also enables us to use our intelligence properly and to see things more realistically.' I was truly delighted to see that this was the single most important managerial lesson my daughter had learnt from me. To value the 'power of calm'. Courage is one thing, calmness is another. To be able to demonstrate courage in a non-aggressive manner is the epitome of civilized existence. It is rewarding to know that one has been able to transmit this lesson to one's children.

*A rare and proud moment:*
*Habil Khorakiwala with His Holiness the Dalai Lama at a Wockhardt Foundation*
*event. Also seen are Nobel Peace Prize laureate, Professor Muhammad Yunus,*
*along with Nafisa and Huzaifa.*

When we started our journey at Wockhardt half a century ago, few would have imagined then that the Indian pharmaceutical industry would emerge as a globally competitive, research-based industry. It is a tribute to both public policy and private enterprise that we are, as an industry, where we are. Many scientists and entrepreneurs have contributed to this process and India has several firms that have made their mark worldwide.

As I look back, I can see that the industry has passed through three distinct phases, each with its own peculiar features. The pharmaceutical industry began in a modest way in the early part of the last century. The Bengal Chemicals and Pharmaceutical Works, set up in 1901 by Acharya Prafulla Chandra Ray, was the first modern drug manufacturing company. In 1935, K.A. Hamied set up Chemical, Industrial and Pharmaceutical Laboratories, now popularly known as CIPLA. In 1941, Dey's Medicine was set up. There were a handful of other such companies, including Sarabhai Chemicals, set up in the 1960s. When we entered the industry, over 80 per cent of all modern medicine was manufactured by Western MNCs. This phase of Western dominance ended in 1970 when Prime Minister Indira Gandhi enacted the Patents Act and encouraged domestic manufacturing.

Large public sector firms like Indian Drugs and Pharmaceuticals Limited (IDPL) and Hindustan Antiobiotics were set up. At the same time, several Indian private companies also began to grow and new ones entered the industry. The second phase of development was from 1970 to 1991. The two markers were the Patents Act of 1970 and the new economic liberalization policies of the P.V. Narasimha Rao government. Both were game changers in their own way. If the Patents Act gave us some protection from MNCs and offered us the breathing space to grow, the liberalization era offered us the opportunity to go global—both for funds and markets. In 1970, over 80 per cent of all pharma products sold in India were manufactured by MNCs. By

1990, this share was down to 20 per cent. Those two were decisive decades for us.

The past half a century has been a period of constant change. The structure of the industry, the policy environment and the nature of competition have changed from one phase to the next. We have succeeded in making use of the opportunities and grown in scope and scale. Few other industrial sectors have experienced such comprehensive change in the policy environment, technology and markets.

Four features make the pharmaceutical sector unique in many ways. First, it has evolved as a genuinely research- and knowledge-based industry. Second, it is an industry dominated by entrepreneurs who are professionals with domain knowledge. From Yusuf Hamied to Parvinder Singh to Anji Reddy and many others, we have had pioneers and leaders with tremendous domain knowledge. That is one reason why the industry's research base has been strong. Third, our customers—the medical fraternity—are highly qualified professionals who know the product they are looking at. An earlier generation of doctors had a Western bias and generally recommended only medicines manufactured by MNCs. Later generations no longer have this bias because they have seen that the products we manufacture are equally good, if not better.

Finally, given the earlier dominance of Western MNCs in the industry, we have a legacy of modern management and marketing practices within the industry and the availability of competent managers. Both have served us well as ownership has moved away from MNCs. MNCs have also played a positive role in bringing in technologies that we have learnt to handle. In short, our industry did not develop in a vacuum. It developed within the parameters defined by these features, imbued by respect for science, for research, for professionals and professionalism. All this has given us a global competitive edge.

In a research- and knowledge-based industry like ours, the key requirement is access to talent. Today, we are able to hire talent globally.

Just as the US is tapping Asian countries for talent in various sectors, we are tapping the West for talent in our fields of research. Many Western scientists are willing to come and work in India. I even have Western talent working for us in Aurangabad. But we are also able to locate research facilities abroad and hire locally. Our research establishment is now truly global.

We are on the threshold of a new phase in the development of the Indian pharmaceutical industry. Going forward, only research-based and globally competitive firms will grow. Indian pharma companies have demonstrated their capacity to evolve, adapt and grow. The industry no longer needs the government's hand-holding nor is it worried about competition from MNCs. Indian pharma is also demonstrating that one can be a global company in every sense of the term, including investing in drug discovery, and yet produce affordable medicine. The only other country that may be able to replicate this model, but has not yet done so, is China. The share of prescription drugs has been growing sharply in China, as modern medicine spreads in a traditional society. In the past two decades the pharmaceutical market in China has grown at an average annual rate of growth of around 17 per cent. Several US drug companies have been based in China for some time now and their business too is growing. Interestingly, several Chinese pharmacists have set up companies in the US, drawing on local talent and selling to the local market in the US. Another country that is emerging as a global player in pharma is South Korea. Presently, their industry is focusing on generics and biosimilars. The South Korean pharma market is expected to touch $20 billion in 2020. The South Korean government has been actively supporting investment in research by local companies and facilitating their growth. In the years to come China and South Korea will emerge as major players in this industry. I am confident that Indian firms too will make their mark globally.

Of course, it will not be an easy ride. The experience of some firms like Ranbaxy has shown this. There will be hurdles ahead, mistakes made. The West will seek to preserve its dominance. But there is also popular public pressure in Western democracies for more affordable medicine and healthcare. They cannot shut their doors to what we are offering and will be able to offer in the years to come. In the 1990s, our mission was to go global. It was a compelling vision and our success gave us immense confidence. Today, our mission is to make a mark in drug discovery, creating a global organization that can deliver on that compelling vision. For the Indian pharmaceutical and biotechnology industry, the best is yet to come.

# Index